Charles Lee

Paul Carah, Cornishman

Charles Lee

Paul Carah, Cornishman

ISBN/EAN: 9783743306554

Manufactured in Europe, USA, Canada, Australia, Japa

Cover: Foto ©Thomas Meinert / pixelio.de

Manufactured and distributed by brebook publishing software
(www.brebook.com)

Charles Lee

Paul Carah, Cornishman

PAUL CARAH CORNISHMAN

BY CHARLES LEE,
AUTHOR OF 'THE
WIDOW WOMAN,' 'A
FOREIGNER IN PEN-
DENNACK,' AND OTHER
STORIES

ILLUSTRATED BY GORDON BROWNE

LONDON: JAMES BOWDEN
10 HENRIETTA STREET,
COVENT GARDEN, W.C.
1898

" ' Et's a token !" he cried.   " There go I, to join my own folk !"

CONTENTS

PAUL CARAH, CORNISHMAN

IN a cloudless autumn sky the sun was dropping to the horizon ; and the moorland, brown and uncomely all day, was beginning to brighten into brief beauty. As the western glow deepened, an answering flush spread over the face of the upland. The withered heather showed unsuspected tints of red and gold ; the pale yellow of the gorse grew to a rich orange ; the pools by the roadside shone and glittered. This dull patch on earth's garment grew lively with colour ; its flat monotony took feature as the shadows lengthened ; and in the lucid air its oppressive immensity shrank into more comfortable bounds. The hills of the mining country to the north advanced their faint green slopes, where flocks of little white cottages

clustered round tall chimneys. Eastward, certain far-off clumps of yellowing elms, planted
as screens before outlying farms, started into
flaming prominence as the warm light caught
their foliage; and they, like the hills, grew
nearer. And in the west, there was the good
sun, floating over the edge of the moor, big
and ruddy, dwarfing all distance. Only to the
southward, where no landmarks were, the moor
still stretched, dim and boundless, to the invisible sea.

Across the moor from north to south ran a
straight, interminable white road. By its side,
at intervals of unrelenting regularity, marched
the rigid telegraph poles, guiding a cluster of
electric nerves down into England's heel. And
southward along the road a young man was
walking briskly, a bundle over his shoulder.
A native meeting him would have set him
down for a foreigner at once. Nothing in his
carriage suggested the rolling gait of the
fisherman, or the cramped weary hobble of the
miner, or the slouch of the farm-hand, who
drags each leg forward with an effort, as if
extricating it from miry clods. He stepped
out alertly, with a spring. His new, ill-fitting
clothes had a foreign cut. When now and

again, without slackening his pace for a moment, he shifted his bundle and took off his hat to wipe his forehead, he exposed a head closely cropped in a style unknown to the English barber. In all his demeanour appeared a lively confidence, not altogether free from bounce. His disengaged arm swung freely— one might almost say with impetuous exaggeration. His broad shoulders stooped forward a little, not as the student's, but as the shoulders of the man who lives in the airy future. For the rest, he was tall, small in the head, bright-eyed, hatchet-faced, but regular of feature, and as lean and muscular as a greyhound.

As he went, he talked and laughed incessantly to himself; and, save when some feature of the landscape momentarily arrested his attention, his thoughts ran far ahead of his feet to his journey's end.

'Seven year! They won't knaw me, not a man of 'em, nor a woman nuther. I belong to have a bit o' fun. My life, what fun I'll have! I won't liv 'em knaw who I am—not at first. I'll spake 'em all by name, an' I'll ask the news o' the rest; an' aw! to see them stickin' their heeds together, an' wonderin', an' p'rapsin', an s'posin'! Good as a play, 'a 'll be. "What manner o' chap may this be," they'll whisper, "wi' the ends of his mustashes like niddles? A foreigner, sure," they'll say. "How should a foreigner belong to knaw all about we? A wisht thing, sure 'nough," they'll say, an' shake their heeds. Aw, what fun! My dear life, what fun!'

He stood still and laughed till the tears ran.

'An' when I liv 'em knaw, there'll be some laffin' an' hand-shakin', an' back-slappin', 'a b'lieve! An' some 'll be makin' out they knawed me all the while; an' 'twill be—"La, how thee'st grawed, Paul!" an'—"Wheer'st been all this while?" an'—"What kind o' locality might this here Ameriky be, na?" An' then there'll be such a givin' an' gettin' o' news as was never knawed afore in Porthvean. I'll pitch 'em some yarns that'll draw the eyes out o' their heeds — lynchin's an' wolf-hunts, an' b'ar hunts, an' prairie fires—why, rabbet et! ef I don't hire Wesley school-room, an' scoop in the town for sixpence a head to hear me yarn! Don't see how I shouldn'. Wan hundred sixpences, say—that's two pound ten. I'll do et, so I will! They'll come, right 'nough—all Porthvean, an' church-town folk, an' downsers

an' lowlanders an' all. An' won't you cut a
dash, Paul, ·my man! You'll be the sinecure,
'a b'lieve. 'A 'll be Paul here an' Paul there all
the while. An' there'll be some fuss an' to-do
'mong the maids, I guess. But I waan't be
catched too quick by they. No, I'll bide queeat
an' look out for a bit of a dowry. Take
money, make money. An' I'll work like a
black man, an' I'll schemie an' schemie, an' 'fore
long I'll be head an' chief, like Jimmy Ellis
'mong the cats. That's me. Rabbet et! my
head's fair buzzin' wi' schemes! I'm the chap
to get along. Work your fingers to the bone,
an' ef you don't work your head overplush,
you'll die in the gift-house. Head an' fingers—
I love to work 'em both. Hard workin' an'
deep thinkin'—that's the life for me. Whoop!
I'll land on top, 'fore die!' he shouted, and
quickened his pace.

A puff of wind, warm and fragrant as new
milk, blew across the moor from the west, and
his thoughts veered round responsive.

'That's good! Furze an' he'th—'tes good
to get the smell of 'em agin arter many years.
There edn' no smell on earth like the smell o'
Cornish ground. An' there edn' no kingdom
on earth to come up to Cornwall; nor no nation

fit to stand up in the sight o' the Cornish nation. "Wan an' all" agin the world. That's we, brothers all! Hoorah for home an' a lovin' welcome, an' pilchers an' saffern an' true friends an' pasties! Gum! I can hear 'em. "Heard the news?" says wan. "How?" says another. "Paul Carah's come home!" "O joyful day! Where is he?" "Down 'pon quay-head." An' off they run. Ten minutes, an' I'll have all the town round me. Aw ess! there'll be feast-day to-day, over to Porthvean.'

By this time he was nearing the limits of the moor. The ground was now broken and undulating. 'Gurgeys,' or low, wide banks of earth faced with stone, fenced the road in on either side. Soon he came upon a solitary cottage, its walls built of stone to the height of a man's breast, and thence upwards of clay. A high-pitched roof of ragged thatch bent like a scowling eyebrow over a low, narrow door and two small windows. Other similar cottages were visible at rare intervals ahead. It was the region of the moor-dwellers or 'downsers,' a strange folk, living lonely lives apart, with their own speech and customs, distinct from those of the miners to the north, of the fishermen to the south and west, and of the agricultural dwellers in the fertile eastern valleys. A giant in stature, the downser inhabits a hut that would be none too large for a pigmy, contracting therein a habitual stoop. Unlike his voluble neighbours, he is slow of speech and morose, as a solitary man is apt to be. He possesses a gun, and eats the flesh of the rabbit, abhorred by all good Cornishmen. But his chief claim to notoriety is that he carries an umbrella to chapel, feast and funeral —not one of your slim effeminate modern affairs of steel and alpaca, but a mighty structure of whale-bone and green cotton, adorned with many patches, stout in the handle, plump of girth, its weight to be calculated by pounds. Elsewhere men leave umbrellas to their womenkind, or must submit to be hailed with the mocking title of 'Downser!' wherever they go. But no man is so bold as to connect the true downser's umbrella with the notion of effeminacy. Its appearance is a sufficient refutation to the stigma.

Beyond the downser's land, the road passed first one farm and then another, with a hollow of green fertility between; then came yet another stretch of moorland. Half-way across this the road divided, one branch turning to the left and keeping across the moor, the other descending sharply to the right, on its way to the coast. This latter road our traveller took.

As soon as the road dipped below the bleak inland level, signs of a kindlier nature appeared. Gorse and heather gave way to pasture and root-crops ; rough-cast stone hedges divided the land into fields ; the road-side banks were topped with thorn-bushes, scantily at first, but soon in serried rows. And their aspect in autumn array, under the warm evening sky, was a thing to wonder at. The sloes, draped from top to foot in livid green lichen and thickly studded with livid blue fruit, the haw-thorns all crimson with haws, the wild roses all orange with hips, the gorse-bushes flaming yellow, the hazels and oak-shrubs in their leaves of every tint, from straw-colour to scarlet— these, mingling and succeeding without inter-mission, made a show of startling, almost unnatural beauty. And they were all alive with bright-coloured birds : robins and chaffinches —which the Cornish boys call copper-finches, because of their burnished metallic breasts— and lemon-crested yellow-hammers in flocks, and titmice in their gay livery of blue and yellow. Sometimes a magpie took its chequered, unsteady flight from the road, or a cinnamon-tinted kestral swooped from a tree-top, or a great clumsy green woodpecker fled, looping its way down between the hedges.

From every bush came a loud chorus of trills and twitterings. They broke on the traveller's ear with the charm of a half-forgotten song of childhood.

'Heark to them singin'! 'Tes good to hear them agin—grey-bird, an' blackbird, an' bush-sparrow. Same auld songs, 'a b'lieve ; *they* don't set no store by new tunes. Makes me feel as ef I was dreamin', like-a-thing. Sim' me 'a edn' but last week I was a lad, minchin' from school to strub nests. Gum! what a hollerin' an' ran-tan they do make! Sim' me they're a-curlin' so to gie me a welcome home, like as ef they knawed. That's et, sure 'nough. Thank'ee, li'll chaps all, thank'ee,' he roared at the top of his voice, laughing boisterously, and waving a gay hand in mock acknowledgment, while a cloud of startled finches rose with a confused rustle of wings and fled before him down the road.

'Pretty li'll chaps! And grand eatin', too, some of 'em! First frosty night I'll get a lantern an' a stick an' go bush-beatin'.

B

I'll get more grey-birds an' starlin's than I can carry. There never was a man to beat me at bush-beatin' in the auld times, lad though I was. An' how? Because I didn' stomp an' fooch about, but manovered an' used my brain. That's me! I'm the wan to manover!'

The sun was below the horizon now, and the lovely Cornish twilight was beginning—a time of purple and orange. The sky receded to immeasurable distances. The earth was half shine, half shadow. The smell of the flowering gorse grew overpowering in its sweetness, and other infinite dewy odours arose; every bush and herb, every clod, exhaled its perfume.

High up and far away in the west, masses of twinkling shadow appeared and swept across the sky, faint, almost lost in the luminous glow. Wheeling in wide circles, they came rapidly nearer, until they were almost overhead. Then they were seen to be a great company of birds — thousands of plovers flown up from their feeding-places in the marshes and by the shore, to sport for a while in the upper air. Round and round they swept, as if animated by one volition, each speck in the mass keeping its exact place in relation to the other specks.

Presently, out of the north came a solitary bird. It was flying low at first, but soon it began to beat upwards with strenuous wings, hurrying to join the flock overhead. The traveller saw it, and laughed joyously.

'That's me,' he cried. 'Et's a token! There go I, to join my own folk. Et's a token, an' meant for me, sure 'nough.'

Higher went the bird, and nearer to its fellows. A few moments more, and it would be merged indistinguishably in the flock, one speck among a thousand. Suddenly the host swerved aside and fled westward again, leaving the one bird far behind. For a while it attempted to follow; but all its efforts brought it no nearer, and soon it dropped earthwards again, and turned and flew back over the road, uttering a plaintive cry.

The man's steps faltered. He stopped, and looked doubtfully behind him. He even turned half about, as if inclined to retrace his way. There was something like terror in his face.

'That's bad,' he murmured; 'I named et for a token, an' a wisht token 'a es. Don't like the looks of en. How should 'a be like that? Don't like the looks of en at all. I've a jealous thought somethin's wrong. I've a mind to turn back.'

He gazed blankly up and down the road, and shivered. Suddenly he flushed crimson, stamping his foot.

'What fullishness!' he exclaimed. 'Paul, my man, how are you so silly? A reg'lar gran'fer you are, with your tokens an' nonsense! What's the doin's of a passel o' birds to you, excep' you're layin' low to shoot 'em or trap em? Forward now! Here's for a glimp o' home 'fore dark!'

He swung round in his original direction, and went quickly on again.

'Wan mile more,' he said aloud. 'I'll be there just between the lights — candle-teenin' time, as they d' say. That's the soshabble time; a man do look for comp'ny most of all when the dark's comin' on. My life! what wisht that bird did squawk! like a lost soul goin' off into the dark alone, poor li'll chap. But 'a wadn' no token for me. How should 'a be so? Pouf! Fullishness!'

Now the road descended steeply, with many windings and abrupt turns. Soon the sea came into view. Paul's excitement grew as he recognised one familiar landmark after another, and all supernatural forebodings were forgotten.

'There's Roseveor Farm, where us lads an' maids used to go wi' ferns on May mornin' to get our bread an' crame. . .

'" Fern, fern, measure your shern,
'" Gie's a morsel o' bread and crame."

'Ha-ha! My life, what queer old ballats we Cornishmen do make up in our heeds! Don't suppose there's another nation on earth do knaw the manin' o' that bit o' dialogue. . .

'Clodgy meadow. Turnups, aha! 'Twas pasture-land in the auld days. Well, mus' look for some changes, s'pose. Maybe Farmer Ivey's dead, an' young Johnny Ivey's got the farm. Johnny always was a bustler, just the chap to upsot creation, an' teel turnups for grass and grass for turnups. Him an' me should get along very well together. Gum! I'll wake the auld place up, so I will! Rabbet et! I'll rent a bit o' land myself, an' teel—an' teel—punkins! Punkins, so I will! Don't s'pose they ever heerd tell o' punkins down here. Gum! in six months I'll have all

Porthvean eatin' punkins for denner, like
reg'lar Yankees! And they'll be fo'ced to buy
'em o' me, an' I'll belong to make a brave lot
o' money, sure 'nough. . .

'Touch-pipe Corner. Hoorah! There's
Penluce lights opening out on Carn Mellyn.
Wan more turn, an' I shall see the auld place
agin. Edn' that a smell o' fish in my nose?
Hoorah! Here 'a es!'

He stood still at a turn in the road. Before
him the land sloped steeply down to a little
tranquil bay, round which the road ran by way
of a low cliff. On the other side of the bay
a horn-shaped spur of the inland hills ran out
into the sea, gradually narrowing and sinking
to a point. Before this little promontory lay
the dark waters of the cove, behind it the dark
waters of the outer sea, and along it from base
to point ran two continuous lines, one above
the other, of white-walled, brown-thatched
cottages. Near the tip of the horn a granite
quay curved a protecting arm round a tiny
pool, above which a dozen boats were drawn
up. Slender threads of smoke ascended into
the calm air from twenty chimneys; lights
already twinkled here and there in the windows;
a small stream spouted over the cliff in a

wavering column, feathered at the base where it struck the rocks; and this was Porthvean—the 'Little Port.'

Paul Carah drew a big breath.

'Don't she look pure an' pretty? Don't knaw o' no such pretty, clane-lookin' li'll town nowheres. Edn' changed a bit, nuther. An' I bet I'll find everybody pitchin' the same auld churrs, an' tellin' the same auld yarns, an' laffin' at the same auld. jokes. *I*'ll give 'em some new wans! *I*'ll wake 'em! But don't she look snug an' pretty? No place like home —that's the sayin'; 'tes a true wan. Don't knaw how I ever came to go away. Edn' no sense or natur' in leavin' the place you're reared to. Aw, my pretty! many's the time I've been sick for a sight of 'ee, 'way out in the prairies! Aw! my eyes are glad an' my heart's joyful to be'old 'ee! Three cheers for home!'

He broke into a run, and did not slacken to a more sober pace until he was down the hill and within hail of the first scattered houses along the cliff.

CHAPTER II

HE IS RECEIVED

THE adult male population of Porthvean was enjoying its evening 'touch pipe' in what served as the town-place, a flat piece of bare ground just beyond the junction of Porthvean's two streets, between the quay-head and the fish-cellars. A dozen weather-beaten, black-bearded men—dark complexions are the rule at Porthvean—were standing in a circle round three others, who were on their hands and knees, playing marbles. Players and spectators were very much in earnest; cries of encouragement, advice, exultation and disappointment were showered incessantly on the heads of the former; occasionally there was a roar of laughter at the antics of one, the wit of the village, a little wrinkled man, well past middle age, who fooled over the game with an ease begotten of long practice, calling his marble pet names, addressing it in alternate terms of piteous entreaty and stern reproof, affecting to clear away invisible straws and pebbles from its path, or pretending to keep it rolling by blowing upon it with distended cheeks and starting eyes. The other two players, a young giant in sea-boots and a blue-eyed coastguardsman, wrapt in the game, paid no heed to his folly, save for an occasional growl at such frivolity over serious matters.

One man, turning from the group for a moment, needing space to slap his thighs and double his body over some crowning stroke of humour, caught sight of a man of unfamiliar gait and appearance, quickly approaching up the street.

''Ware foreigner!' he exclaimed.

The three who sprawled on the ground sprang to their feet, kicking the marbles away out of sight. All faced in the direction of the stranger, looking somewhat abashed. Put on its mettle, Porthvean would be the first to defend the dignity of its favourite game; but foreigners have been known to laugh at the spectacle of grown men playing marbles, and 'proud Porthvean,' as the neighbours call it, is morbidly sensitive to ridicule.

'Who is he?' went round.

The wit was tapping his forehead. His memory for faces was famous.

'I should knaw that man,' he said, 'for the way 'a do step out, all over the place to wance. Stand back, soase, an' gie my brain room. Where have I seen arms a-swingin' like that before? Ah! now I can make out the face of en I d' knaw en, f'rall his mush-tashes. Edn' no foreigner, Sammy. Porth-vean man, sure 'nough. That's Paul Carah, or I'm a Dutchman.'

'Paul Carah? So 'a es — Jim's right. What's brought en back again? — no good, I'll be bound. Always was a mischievous lemb, Paul was—pushin' an' hollerin'.'

'Haul' tongue!' said Jim. 'Here 'a es.'

Paul was advancing towards them, striving to keep his countenance set in such a blank frame as a stranger might be supposed to wear, but betraying by certain twitches about the mouth and eyes his anticipatory enjoyment of the situation as he imagined it. While still some yards away he accosted the group.

'Good evenin', friends all. Can you tell

me—this li'll place '—waving his hand to the houses—' edn' Porthvean the name of en?'

Looks of astonishment were interchanged. Then some seized the point, and grinned. Evidently Paul counted on being unrecognised, and intended to play off a joke on them. The slower ones followed in comprehension, and growled, having a distaste for banter.

'Liv en to me,' whispered the little man they called Jim. 'I'll settle en.'

He ran forward, cringing and bowing.

'Ess, your honour,' he said in tones of exaggerated humility, 'Porthvean's the name of our poor li'll place, sure 'nough. Edn' a fitty place for quality to set foot in, but you're welcome, all the same.'

Paul chuckled inwardly. The joke was successful. But what were the others grinning at?

'Thank 'ee,' he said. 'Edn' a bad li'll place. Maybe I'll stop here for a bit, ef I can find accommodation.' The big word was rolled out with an indescribable relish.

'Aw, plenty o' that,' said the other, 'plenty. We haven' got what you may call a first-class hotel; but there's a tidy li'll inn up above there. I wouldn' rec'mend the

wines to your honour, though they're good
'nough for we ; but the beds are capital.
Edn' they capital beds, naibours ? '

'Capital, sure 'nough,' they chorused. ' Aw,
Jim's the chap ! Pitch into en, Jimmy ! '

There was a sound of suppressed laughter.
Paul peered suspiciously into their faces, which
suddenly stiffened into preternatural gravity.

' Or ef the inn don't suit 'ee,' continued Jim
without moving a muscle, 'there's a commo-
jous li'll pigs-crow in my garne. I can turn
the auld sow out, an' put down fresh litter, an'
'a 'll be just the place for your honour.'

A roar of laughter interrupted him. Paul
glared furiously from one to another. Then
he turned pale, clenched his fists, and stepped
up to one of the group—the biggest for choice
—him who elected to play marbles in sea-boots.

' Look, Bob Rowe ; ef you don't stop
grizzlin' at me, I'll scat your ugly face to
jowds ! '

' Wadn' no use, Paul Carah ! ' gasped Jim,
the tears running down his face. ' I knawed
'ee, soon's I set eyes upon 'ee. Ha-ha ! '

' Take off thy coat, Bob Rowe,' yelled
Paul, ' ef thou'rt a man ! Take off thy coat
an' stick up thy fistes ! '

'Don't see how I should do that,' said the young giant good-temperedly. 'What's your 'nnoyance wi' me in p'tickler?'

Paul was dancing with rage. 'Don't care who 'a es, then! I'll take the whole dirty-fingered crowd! Come on, my scrapers of oarweed an' menders o' stinkin' crab-pots. I'll smash the lot of 'ee!'

Angry voices arose. Some of the men began to close round Paul.

''Ere, that'll do,' said a quiet-spoken old man, who had hitherto stood aloof. 'Liv the man alone. Don't 'ee see he's mazed with anger, an' don't knaw what he's doin'. An' you, Paul Carah, fit an' put on your coat agin. Shame upon 'ee to be wantin' to smash folks' faces, an' you not in the place five minutes, just because the joke's agin you when you thought fur'n to be the other way round. Make a joke, take a joke.'

Paul's anger died down as it had blazed up, a fire of straw. He began to laugh.

'No offence, naibours. The auld chap's right. I'm quick to anger, but et don't last long—that's me. I thought to have a bit o' fun wi' 'ee, but you 'uns got in ahead, an' that made me mad. I can take a joke so well as

any, gie me time. An' 'a wadn' such a bad
joke, nuther. Turn the auld sow out, eh?
That edn' bein' polite to a lady, an' I wouldn'
do no s'ch thing, not I—ha-ha!'

'That's very well,' muttered one of the
men; 'but we don't want no foreigners comin'
round profanin' over us an' callin' us dirty-
fingered.'

'That's so, Steve,' said another, and several
nodded assent.

'I edn' no foreigner,' said Paul, quickly and
hotly.

''Course you edn',' interposed the peace-
maker, 'though you've been away a brave bit
of a while, an' a brave long way, too, I've no
doubt.'

'You're right there, uncle!' exclaimed Paul,
forgetting his wrath, and eagerly seizing the
opportunity to yarn. 'Half over the States
I've been, an' into Canady—v'yaged thousands
o' miles, 'a b'lieve, workin' at my trade, sometimes—I'm a mason, you d' knaw, like father
was—an' sometimes trappin', an' lumberin', an'
carpenterin', an' loadin' steamers, an' doin'
'most everythin' you can think upon. Rabbet
et! I've seen life, I can tell 'ee, an' had some
fun too.'

'An' how ded 'ee come to come back?'
asked his interlocutor.

'I'll tell 'ee. 'A wadn' but a month ago I
was up to Columbus, Ioway, an' I met a
Cornishman there ; Camborne man he was, an'
Bill Hosken the name of en. Well, 'course we
got yarnin' 'bout home ; an' Hosken, he said to
me, "I'm on my way back to the auld place."
"How?" I asked en. "Like this," said Hosken.
"I had a dream t'other night, an' I dreamt I
was dead an' my bones laid out here ; an' I was
that wretched at the thought o' lyin' alone
away from home, that I couldn' rest in my
grave," said Hosken. "My sperit walked,"
said he ; "that's how I dreamt et. An' I woke
sheverin' an' asked myself—how ef this dream
should come true? How ef I should be fo'ced
to lie here alone 'mong strangers till Judgment
Day? An' when the Day do come, who's to
knaw me for a true Cornishman, 'mong a parcel
o' Yankees? An' then," said Hosken to me,
"I thought 'pon the queeat li'll simmitery 'pon
the hill at home, an' the peaceful white grave-
stones, an' the maids comin' up of a Sunday,
an' settin' an' chattin' wi' their sweet Cornish
talk over the heads o' the dead folk—an' says
I—'Pick up, Bill Hosken, an' go thee'st home,

'fore 'tes too late.'" That's what Hosken said
to me, 'way out in Ioway. An' I said to en—
"Fullishness! Plenty o' time 'fore die." An''a
said to me—"The Lord alone do knaw 'bout
that, soase." Naibours,' continued Paul, lowering his voice, "a wadn' but next day, Hosken
was steppin' 'pon the cars, homeward bound,
when his foot slipped, an' down he went, an'
the cars went over en. Aw, 'twas wisht, I can
tell 'ee. An' they buried en, so well as they
could in their foreign fashion—no procession
nor hymns nor nothin', an' the box drawn by
horses in a carriage, foreign way, an' me the
only Cornishman that followed en. An' as I
followed, I kep' sayin' to myself—"Him to-day,
me to-morrow. 'Tes. a token for 'ee, Paul,"
said I; an' I went back an' put up my things,
an' home I came, right away.'

Even the antagonistic spirits were awed to
silence by a tale which touched their inmost
feelings so nearly.

'Wisht, sure 'nough,' said the old man,
'an' I don't blame 'ee for comin' back arter
that. But I'm thinkin' you'll find our li'll place
brave an' dull arter all your ticklish v'yages an'
perils by land an' say. Edn' much do happen
in *our* queeat li'll nationality.'

'Aw, don't trouble 'bout that,' said Paul. 'Don't matter where I may be, things are bound to happen. Get a dozen folks round 'ee an' you've got friends an' foes before long ; an' what more do 'ee want to make things brisk ? I often think to myself, this here life below's like settin' down to a denner ; work's your pasty, an' play's your tart ; friends are your butter an' sugar, an' foes are your mustard an' salt. Pasty without salt's a poor look-out, an' so's life without foes. Gum ! *I* do want to fight *my* way ; *I* don't want to slide along— that's me. Put me 'pon a light-ship or put me in London town—don't make no difference. I'm happy, gie me wan to shake hands wi' an' wan to shake fists at. That's the kind o' chap *I* am, naibours. I liv you all knaw ; there edn' nothin' secret 'bout *my* natur'. An' now you d' all knaw how to take me.'

He threw his chest out and looked round on them with beaming self-satisfaction. They returned his looks in various ways, some with neutral faces, one or two with friendly approval, several with half-veiled hostility.

The little man they called Jim spoke, his head on one side, his eyes twinkling with cunning.

C

'That's right,' he said in tones of hearty approbation. 'You're a smart chap, I can see, an' a queeat, proper-be'aved wan, the sort we all like. But this here Ameriky, now,' he continued, his head almost resting on his shoulder, his eyes narrowing to mere slits, 'et's a fine locality, so I've heerd tell, with its gold-mines an' silver-mines. There's a power o' money to be picked up there, 'a b'lieve ; an' they that do g' out there do mostly come back brave an' rich—edn' that so ? '

'Aw ess, a fine country, a tremenyous fine country,' replied Paul ; 'an' the dollars do fly about there like yellow-birds in a rick-yard. But et wants a smart chap to catch 'em, same as anywhere else.'

'An' you're a smart chap, eh ? Dedn' I say so ? ' said Jim.

Paul laughed.

'I take your manen,' he said. 'But you see they're all smart chaps out there. Still, I haven' done so bad—haven' made my fortune azackly, but I've got about enough to stem between the seasons an' make a start wi' nex' year. That's about et, I reckon.'

'An' what kind of a start might you be thinkin' o' makin', now ? ' pursued Jim. 'Edn' much mason-work to do hereabouts, ef that's your notion.'

'Pouf! Mason-work!' exclaimed Paul, waving a disgusted hand away. 'I've done wi' such truck for good. 'A edn' the trade to suit me no longer—edn' no fun in it, hammerin' away at gashly auld stones. I d' want a fightin', bustlin' trade, I do; an' where's the fight in a block o' granite? You may hammer en, an' hammer en, but 'a waan't hammer back. You work upon 'm all day an' go home, an' come back nex' day—an' there 'a es, just the same as you left en. No, 'a don't take my fancy at all. V'riety—that's what I belong to look for—v'riety, an' a spice o' danger, an' a chanst to schemie, an' a chanst to venture my luck. Good-bye auld stones! Three cheers for fish!'

There was a stir of surprise.

'Fish!' exclaimed one. 'Don't 'ee tell me, Paul Carah, that you've come back here to Porthvean to go fishin'!'

'Ess, so I have,' replied Paul. 'Tell 'ee, naibours, I've had et in my mind a brae long time. An' where's the wonder? There edn' no occypation I d' knaw of to compare wed'n for fun. Edn' that so? Edn' you fightin' an'

schemin' all the while agin the winds an' tides?
Edn' you settin' your wits all the while agin the
crafty auld crabs an' conger? 'Tes battle,
battle, all the time. An' I'm a Porthvean man,
—et's in my blood, 'a b'lieve. Ess, there's salt
in my veins; the smell o' salt water's life to
me. Many's the time, out there 'pon the
prairies, I've been reg'lar sick wi' longin' arter
the say. An' now I'm back, I'll live and die wi'
the sound of en in my ear. Hoorah for a fisherman's life! Shake han's, naibours all, an' wish
me luck!'

No one advanced to take his proffered hand;
but he was not to be baulked. He grasped the
fist, first of Jim the wit, who shook it with
burlesque energy, and then of the friendly old
man, who pressed it kindly, and said :—

'Good luck ti' 'ee, soase. But et's a poor
trade.'

The others shrank back.

'I wouldn' shake han's, ef I were you, Paul
Carah,' said one. 'We are a dirty-fingered
lot.'

Muttered words passed from one to another.
The man who had been addressed as Steve
stepped forward, scowling unpleasantly.

'Look!' he said. 'Better fit you go back

where you come from, an' liv us to mend our stinkin' crab-pots in peace. You're a brae fine chap, no doubt, an' do knaw so much as a Devonshire lawyer, but we edn' got no room for 'ee here—catchin' our fish an' snatchin' the bread out of our mouths. Bad 'nough to have these here trawlers comin' an' scrapin' our grounds bare, an' Porthellick men sneakin' up on dark nights without a lantern to prick our cuttle. But to have a foreigner comin' and usin' our quay, and sellin' our fish in our own town—'tes too much, a brae sight too much!'

Several chorused assent.

'You're right, Steve. So 'a es.'

Paul's face, blank with amazement at first, began to work with anger. His fists clenched, and every muscle of him quivered. But the force of the shock thrust him out beyond wrath. His hands dropped open by his sides, and he sat down on the edge of a boat, limp and despondent.

'Here's a pretty welcome home!' he exclaimed. 'An' I've been dreamin' night an' day, seven year, o' the time when I should come back to where I was reared to, an' those I was reared with. "Home!" I'd say, an' my heart 'ud jump. So home I come, an' you—an' you —aw! 'tes hard!'

He leapt up and blazed. 'But here I am, an' here I stick! I edn' wan to be druv away by bad words. I edn' wan to shirk a fight: you'll find that out before long! Wan an' all agin me—I'll hauld my own! What I d' say, I d' stick to, mind that! That's me, Paul Carah, fisherman o' Porthvean. Fisherman! dost hear, thou bussa?'—This to Steve. 'I'll catch more fish in a week than ever you stole in a year — an' that's a brave lot, I'll be bound. *Your* fish, say you! Is the say yourn? Did 'ee salt et yourself? Maybe you keep the winds put up in tatie-sacks in your cellar, an' squeeze 'em out to suit yourself! Your fish! So much mine as yourn, 'a b'lieve. I'm a Porthvean man so much as you; an' ef I wadn', 'twould be all the same. Here I am, an' here I stick, an' fish so long as I've a mind to—an' so for you!'

'Simmin' to me, you waan't get much profit out of en,' Steve muttered darkly, and moved away, followed by the others one by one, until Paul was left standing alone with the friendly old man.

There was a brief silence. Then the old man put his hand on Paul's shoulder.

'Well, soase,' he said, 'for a smart man, you've made a bit of a mess of et.'

Paul was still quivering with rage.

'Don't care!' he cried. 'I edn' to be putt upon by nobody. I ask 'ee, have I been trated the way I should be, a Cornishman, and a Porth-vean man, come back to my own folk, my heart a-swellin' wi' love an' kind feelin' for 'em all? That's how I felt as I come up the street, an' now I could smash the lot of 'em.'

'You'd be a smarter man ef you dedn' gie way to anger so quick,' said the other. 'We're a queeat lot, livin' harmonial, more or less; an' when you come down with a plop an' a splash, like a g'eat gannet in a school o' mullet, you started us a bit. What you belong to do now is to lie low for a bit, an' let us get used ti' 'ee, like-a-thing. Then you'll find us soshabble enough.'

'Look, uncle!' said Paul eagerly. 'Don't 'ee get a wrong notion o' my char'cter. I'm hot sometimes, but that's because I'm warm always. I may gie way to anger, but I don't seek quarrels, an' I don't bear a grudge. Only, wance let me find a man be'avin' deceitful or mean, an' I don't trust that man agin, nor have dealin's wed'n. That's me. Edn' no sin in gettin' angry. I wouldn' be one o' your cold-blooded toads, blawed up wi' my own conceit. I'm warm all the while—a true friend, an open enemy. But don't ask me to act agin my char'cter, an' hide my natur' under my shirt. Plaised or angry, I must out wed'n. I waan't say ef 'tes a fault or a virtue—'tes the way I'm built, that's all.'

The old man regarded Paul with a kindly twinkle.

'Don't pat your temper on the back too much,' he said gently, and relapsed into silent thought.

It was dark by now, and the air was chilly. All was silent in the village, and the murmur of the village's great neighbour stole nearer through the quiet. There were sleepy mutterings from the tide on the sand, and the sound of softly clapping hands and breaths drawn with a hiss from the wakeful waves on the outer rocks. The stream that fell over the cliff grew confident, and babbled moorland secrets aloud.

'Where goin' 'night?' said the old man suddenly.

'Don't know, I'm sure,' Paul replied in dejection. 'I looked for wan o' they chaps to offer to take me in; but now, mus' g' up to the inn, s'pose. Don't sim much like home, where you're fo'ced to do that.'

'Look!' said the other. 'How shouldn' 'ee come back home-along wi' me? You mind me, don't 'ee? I'm Ben Jose, an' I live out there to East Corner wi' my daughter Jennifer. You mind Jennifer Jose?'

'Ess, sure,' said Paul. 'Red-haired maid, edn' 'a?'

Ben Jose winced.

''Tes brave an' pretty-lookin' hair, I d' think,' he said rather sharply. 'Some do call et red, 'a b'lieve. 'A edn' red to my mind. But will 'ee come? I've took a fancy ti' 'ee, an' that's the truth; an' ef you like to stop on with us, my daughter 'll make ye comfortable. Come now, will 'ee?'

'That I will, an' thank 'ee kindly!' exclaimed Paul. 'You're my man, you are—a true Cornishman, wan o' the good auld sort. You an' me should get along fine together. Shake han's, uncle; 'tes a bargain!'

'That's right!' cried Mr Jose heartily, as they grasped hands. 'An' now, come along an' see for a bit o' supper. This cauld air do make one rawnish.'

Together they passed through the village, and back along the cliff road by the way Paul had arrived. They turned up the road inland for a few yards, and then Mr Jose stopped by a gate.

'Here we are,' he said. 'Welcome home, Paul Carah!'

CHAPTER III

HE IS INSTALLED

WITHIN the gate, they were in a narrow path with dwarfish trees on either hand. Gnarled branches that writhed and zig-zagged in every unexpected way were dimly visible about them. Paul's foot trod on something round and firm. It burst and was crushed beneath his weight, and a pleasant odour of apples rose to his nostrils. Further on, a feeble trace of light fell on the path, and the outline of a house loomed up. They passed a lighted, curtained window, and stopped at a door framed about with the bare twigs of a climbing plant. The old man lifted the latch, and they entered.

The door opened immediately into a room. A burning candle stood on the table by the window, but the warm light that flooded the room came from the fringle. Does the fringle exist out of Cornwall? In the old farmhouses up country the great open hearths are still found; houses of recent date are furnished with 'slabs,' or common-place kitchen ranges, but many cottages dating from about a century back possess fireplaces in the nature of a compromise between the two, and such was the case here. The fireplace was divided down the middle by a partition-wall; on one side was a diminutive slab, with an oven: on the other was a big door—like a cupboard door—of tarred wood, flush with the wall. When swung back, it disclosed an open hearth, raised some eighteen inches above the level of the ground. The concrete floor had a small grating in the centre, over which stood a 'brandis,' or triangular frame of iron. A small oblong tunnel running under the grating provided the necessary draught.

The fringle door was open, and bending over it, her face and figure lit up by a great fire of sticks, was a young girl, engaged in stirring the contents of a big pot set on the brandis. She turned as they entered.

'Daddy dear,' she said softly; and then her eyes rested with calm inquiry on Paul.

Paul was staring—frankly and undisguisedly staring.

'My life, you're a strange wan, an' no mistake!' he said to himself.

A foreigner might have found another and a more complimentary epithet to fit her with, but Paul's notions of feminine beauty did not go beyond those of local currency. According to these, the ideal fitty-looking maid should be complexioned in black and red, or in gold and pink. Such abnormal features as ruddy chestnut hair, cheeks of a dead privet whiteness which no amount of exposure to Cornish weather could tan, and great wide-set eyes of a colour which no mortal could give a name to, were things to wonder at, to shrink from, even, as wisht and witch-like—certainly not to admire.

Assuredly there was something wisht and unearthly in her appearance, as she stood half turned away from the crackling blaze, which danced fitfully in her eyes, and made of her hair an aureole of flame. And what strange brewage was she preparing in that great pot?

Ben Jose explained the situation to her, and submitted his plan for harbouring Paul. Did it meet her approval?

She inclined her head without speaking.

'Plaised to meet 'ee agin, Jennifer,' said Paul in his loud voice. 'I mind 'ee very well as a li'll maid, no higher than the table. La, what a fine g'eat wench you've grawed to! You an' me are goin' to get along very well together, edn' that so?' he added with a conquering grin.

She was queer to look at, certainly; but gallantry came easily to him, and even the plainest maids are known to be susceptible to it.

She turned her great eyes upon him again, and the grin faded.

'That's as may be,' she said. She said it simply, without any offensive inflection, but he felt himself effectually snubbed.

'I don't take ti' 'ee at all, my dear, plaise sure,' he said to himself, and turning away, began to examine his new surroundings, while the girl, at a hint from her father, set about preparing the table for a meal.

It was the typical Porthvean kitchen. Four doors opened out from it: one was that by which Paul and his host had entered, the next in order was the door of the best room, a third communicated by a passage with the larder, and the fourth gave access to the dark, steep staircase which led to the upper rooms. From the beams of the 'planchin'' or flooring overhead depended various hooks and loops of twine, on which were hung — a sou'wester; a short-handled besom, home-made from 'griglans' or dried heather-stalks; a bundle of dried mugwort, Porthvean's sovereign specific against colds; an ostrich egg, hardly ever absent from the inventory of a Cornish fisherman's dwelling—why, no one can say; a stuffed gull, with its wings outspread; what appeared to be a rolling-pin fashioned out of blue glass—ornamental, like the gull; a pair of pattens; an ancient silver watch, rotund, immense, not to be accommodated by any modern pocket; and a canary in a circular wire cage.

All these articles were hung at a height calculated to suit the convenience of Mr Jose, who was not a tall man. For a person of Paul's stature, progress about the room necessitated nearly as much delicate ordering of one's steps as in an egg-dance.

Paul's keen eyes roved among the forest of paraphernalia, taking stock. So far, all was ordinary, eliciting no comment. But his attention was at once arrested when his glance fell

on the walls of the room. Instead of the usual
adornment of lugubrious funeral cards and
chromolithographic offerings from local tradesmen, the walls were literally papered with
maps—maps without end, maps of the globe
in hemispheres, of the globe on Mercator's
projection, of the four continents and Australia,
of the British Isles, of nearly every country
under the sun—all painted in the gaudiest
colours, and occupying every inch of available
space from the ceiling nearly down to the floor.

Paul uttered a cry of enlightenment.

'I mind 'ee now!' he exclaimed. 'You're
Jog'fry Jose, to be sure you are!'

'That's me,' replied his host with a bashful
laugh. 'Jog'fry's my delight, an' the makin'
o' maps my divarsion. What you d' see has
been the work of evenin's for a matter o'
twenty year. Edn' bad, are they?—make the
room look brave an' gay, 'a b'lieve,' he murmured with modest pride.

Paul was up by the walls, examining.

'Grand, sure 'nough!' he exclaimed. 'Noble
maps they are, to be sure, an' drawed off to
perfection.'

They were really very well done, the outlines
firm and accurate, the names printed in with ex-

quisite neatness. The severe critic in carto-
graphy might have considered it a blemish that
wherever Cornwall was included in any one of
them, it was with considerable magnified proportions, the effect being to give old England
the appearance of suffering from a severe attack
of gout in the foot. But this unconscious
glorification of his native county by the artist,
if it was a fault, was at least a pardonable one,
to be noted with respectful sympathy.

Paul lit on a map of North America, and
uttered a cry of delight.

'Here! look! the States an' Canady, all
complete! My life, how 'andsome you've
drawed 'em off! New York — there's New
York; that's where I landed. An' Boston—I
shipped home from Boston. An' Chicago—I've
been there. An' there's Lake Erie; you've
painted en blue, and blue 'a es, sure 'nough.
Gum! You couldn' ha' putt en in more c'rrect,
not ef you'd been there yourself! An' Ioway
—jiggered ef you haven' made en green!
That's Ioway, right 'nough — mostly pasture
land, so green's the colour fur'n. My ivers! ef
this don't beat everythin' I've heard tell on!'
he cried in ecstasy.

'Now I'll see for Columbus,' he continued.

D

'Columbus, Ioway, that's where I come from last.   You've got en in somewheres, I'll be bound.'

He peered closely into the map.

'Caan't make en out,' he said.   'Fetch the candle, uncle.   I belong to sarch en out, ef 'tes here.'

Mr Jose was fidgeting nervously.

'I don't think—I caan't mind—' he hesitated —'sim' me that there place wadn' marked in my maps.'

'Not Columbus, Ioway!' exclaimed Paul in reproachful astonishment.

'I—I can't mind en,' stammered the old man, terribly disconcerted.   'Is—is et much of a place?'

'Much of a place?' echoed Paul indignantly. 'A reg'lar city!   Five churches an' a jail, all complete!   Why, there'll be a dozen houses at least in that town what I did the mason-work for, myself; an' I wadn' there but six months. Twelve houses in six months—that'll tell 'ee!'

'I'm vexed,' said Mr Jose humbly.   'But,' he added eagerly, 'ef you'll show me the locality of en, I'll put en in.'

'So I will,' promised Paul.   'But I wouldn be vexed.   Come to think of et, Columbus is a new town—brand new. Maybe 'a wadn' there when you drawed your map. They're bustlers out in the States, I can tell 'ee.'

'Well,' said Mr Jose, 'I don't hauld with all this buildin' o' new cities an' upsottin' o' maps. How don't they stick to the auld towns, like we do in Cornwall? There's Afriky, now; you caan't think the sight o' trouble Afriky's guv me. Always wan o' these traveller chaps a-muzzlin' round, sarchin' out new localities. An' I hear tell of 'em in the paper, an' I don't knaw where to put 'em. 'Tes terrible decom-posin', so 'a es. But come,' he continued, shaking off his gloom, 'maybe you'd like to see my tayckle, what I work with.'

He went to a shelf and carefully took down a small pile of papers and boxes. There was a cheap school atlas, dating from twenty years back, the pages much inked and soiled. There were several sheets of cartridge paper, one, which was nailed with tacks to a board, having a half-finished map traced upon it. There was a child's colour-box, and another box which contained bottles of red and black ink, a pair of compasses, a ruler, and three or four mapping pens. With his great horny fingers, swollen and malformed by years of hard toil, he took up his delicate implements one by one, handling them tenderly, and gazing on them with fond eyes, as he expatiated on their various uses, and discussed the dignity of the carto-graphic art.

'Some do come in here,' he said, 'an' say to me, "Ben, how don't 'ee have stately pictures 'pon your walls, like we, 'stead o' these bistly auld maps?" But what I say is—maps do always tell the truth; there edn' no deception in maps, they're sound doctrine all the while. But pictures—pictures are lyin' trade, an' meant to deceive the eye. Take a picture of a place —Porthvean, say—an' look upon 'm. Brave an' pretty, say you, an' wonderful like; might be the auld town itself. But 'a edn' no s'ch thing, I say—edn' but a pretence an' a decep-tion. An' 'a don't *tell* 'ee nothin'—don't give 'ee no manner of *information*—don't give 'ee nothin' but just what you can see for yourself. "Which is *Fisherman's Arms* an' which is Wesley Chapel?" you ask. Picture waan't tell 'ee. What's the use of en, I ask? Pictures! I d' knaw all about 'em; I've seed 'em concoctin'. There was a young artis' chap goin' round laast summer with his paintin' tayckle, an I used to keep an eye 'pon 'm.

Well, you wouldn' believe! The scand'lous way that chap 'ud go alterin' an' improvin' the Lord's handiwork, puttin' in a tree here, an' missin' out a stone there, an' manufacturin' sheep an' things out of his own brain! I'd say to him, "How come you to put trees there where there edn' none?" "That's to improve the composition," he say. "Young man," I said to 'm, "simmin' to me, drawing lies is 'most as bad as tellin' 'em." That made en laff fit to scat his sides. But I knawed I was right. No lyin' pictures for me. I stick to maps.'

'Down wi' pictures! Hoorah for maps!' shouted his sympathetic auditor.

And now Jennifer dished up the contents of the portentous pot, which proved to be nothing more *outré* than lickie-soup—a broth of leeks and turnips, richly flavoured with lumps of fat pork. From the oven she took a potato cake, 'cripsed over' a beautiful brown; and she lifted the tea-pot from the slab where it had been gently simmering and stewing all day long; and she filled the cups with that potent liquor, bitter and black, which to the un-seasoned Englishman is poison, but mother's milk to the brave sons of Cornwall. And so they sat down to sup.

After supper came touch-pipe time, and Paul, producing a corn-cob from his pocket, with— 'There, did 'ee ever see the like o' that? That's what we do smokie wi' in the States'— launched out into a tangle of yarns about forests and prairies, and cyclones and black men, and the wonderful smartness of the Yankee, and the still more wonderful smartness of a certain Porthvean man, who had fought and schemed for seven years beyond the seas with unvarying success. How he shouted, and smote the table, till the tea-cups, timidly starting away from him, had to be rescued from imminent leaps over the extreme edge! How he slapped his host's knees till they tingled again!

Mr Jose was a model listener. In two minutes his pipe was out, and he never thought to light it again. His laughter, his ejaculations of sympathy and astonishment, came pat in the right places. Jennifer sat silent in a corner, and never raised her eyes from her knitting. Presently, when Paul paused and looked round at the end of a blood-curdling yarn, she had vanished.

'Hullo!' he exclaimed. 'Where's the maid?'

'Gone up to her chamber, 'a b'lieve,' said Mr Jose. 'She's as queeat 'pon her feet as a cat.'

'H'm,' said Paul. 'She don't set much store by my yarns, simminly.' He was quick to scent a slight.

'Jennifer never was much of a wan for comp'ny,' apologised Mr Jose. 'She's a good li'll maid, an' a lovin' daughter ; but I'm vexed sometimes the way she do keep by herself all the while. 'A edn' natural at her age. Look now, she's a fitty-lookin' maid, edn' 'a ?'

'Never see nobody like her,' said Paul truthfully.

'That's what I say,' exclaimed the other, highly delighted. 'Aw, I'm sure, gie the chaps a chanst, they'd be buzzin' round her like flies about a honey-pot. But no : she waan't consort wi' none of 'em—says she don't wish none. Don't seem natural in a maid, say I.'

He eyed Paul wistfully.

'I'd be brave an' glad,' he continued, 'to see some smart, well-be'aved chap comin' round a-courtin' of her. Don't 'ee go s'posin' I want to get rids of her. She's the apple o' my eye, li'll Jennifer is ; an' my heart'll be sore to lose her. But 'tes accordin' to natur' for fathers to

be fo'ced to give up them that they've reared
an' tended to the first chap that comes along
I wouldn' grumble, nor I wouldn' set myself
agin natur'. All I do want is to see my
Jennifer be'avin' like other maids. 'Tes the
law o' nations for young people to walk by
twos an' not by ones. Besides, I'm an auld
man, an' what's to become of her when I'm
gone? I'll tell 'ee somethin',' he added in a
low tone, bending forward and plucking Paul's
sleeve. 'There's a bit of a dowry savin' up
for her, an' 'tes more than they think for over
to Porthvean. Two hundred pound! How
the chaps 'ud come scrammin' round, ef they
knawed! Two hundred pound, an' a fitty
maid, an' wan that can cook an' mend clo'es
wi' the best of 'em! What d'ye say to that?'

He peered anxiously into Paul's face, striving
to read the effect of his words there. Through
Paul's brain passed the mental equivalent of a
wink. 'Twas plain enough what the old chap
was after. But he was not going to let, himself
go too cheap.

'A brave lot o' money, sure 'nough,' he
said indifferently. 'Well, I was goin' to tell
'ee the way I used to catch these here wolves
out in Canady.'

Mr Jose sank back with a sigh of disappointment, and one of Paul's best yarns was wasted on unnoticing ears. Politeness kept his eyes fixed with seeming attention on his guest, but his thoughts wandered, and his interjected comments were forced, and mostly inappropriate. Deprived of the necessary stimulus of appreciative attention, the current of Paul's narrative slackened, and presently sank completely out of sight in a series of bottomless yawns. The old man accepted with alacrity a suggestion that bed was a desirable place for a man who had walked more miles that day in a shorter time than ever man had walked before. He willingly led his guest upstairs to a low whitewashed chamber, hung with an overflow exhibition of maps. The perfume of apples which pervaded the room was accounted for, when Mr Jose lifted what Porthvean calls the petticoat of the bed, and displayed the year's crop of his little orchard heaped up beneath, while inviting Paul, if he should chance to wake up hungry in the night, to slip his hand underneath and help himself. And so, with no more words, they got to bed.

CHAPTER IV

HE MAKES A FRIEND

WHEN Paul awoke it was broad daylight, and the air about him was vibrating with the shrill notes of the canary in the room below. He was alone; Mr Jose had risen, and slipped away without disturbing him. He lay a while, lapped in the complacent comfort of the first waking moments, a state so far transcending, for pleasurable emotion, all others that life has to offer us, that to the philosophical inquirer the act of getting up, achieved by thousands daily with unfailing regularity, seems to partake in no small degree of the miraculous, infinitely exceeding as it does all that can be credited to mere human resolution.

Originally there had been two windows to the room ; but one had been blocked up in the days of the French wars, when the window tax pressed heavily on poor folk. Through the remaining one, which was small, low, and set deep in the thick outer wall, Paul, as he lay in bed, could see the village, as in a picture-frame, shining white in the early sun, and the dark tranquil quay-pool lying beneath it. White jackets moved up and down the quay; gulls floated across on white wings above it. A peaceful little world it seemed, the little world he was to conquer. His thoughts wore the rosy-hued garments of the morning. As he lay lapped in idle warmth, all achievement seemed possible to him. His unpromising reception of the night before was a thing to make light of. He would work and scheme; his affable manners would win all hearts; his successful fishing would inspire respect; and Jennifer and her two hundred pounds lay ready to his hand, if he chose to pick them up.

He sprang out of bed and dressed with all speed, eager to embark on his conquering career without delay. Downstairs he clattered. There was no one in the kitchen; 'twas an excellent opportunity for inspecting his new surroundings. Round about he went, peeping into boxes and canisters, trying on the sou'-wester, taking inventory of cupboard and coal-

hole in a spirit of boyish curiosity. He penetrated into the larder, unhooked the side of
bacon which hung there, and made a mental
guess at its weight. He uncovered the big
earthen pan which stood on the floor, and
smacked his lips to find it packed to the brim
with pilchards, white as lilies, and generously
sprinkled with glistening salt. Then, emerging
from the larder, he peeped into the parlour, a
tiny room, but one which contrived to crowd
within its narrow limits as much angular dis-
comfort as any company-receiving apartment in
the kingdom. Five rigid, slippery-seated
chairs were ranged in uncompromising order-
liness against the walls, each with its white,
knobby antimacassar hung symmetrically over
the back. On the mantelshelf stood shoulder
to shoulder a formidable array of glass and
china ornaments—awesome shapes, misbegotten
of nightmares, patterns which no human
creature, however depraved, could have con-
ceived without diabolical aid, colours that
shrieked like lost souls in torment. In the
middle of the room was a small round table,
veneered to pass for mahogany, one-legged,
and claw-footed. On the table a large wool
mat, green and yellow; on the large mat a

small mat, blue and orange. On the small mat an erection of artificial fruit under a glass shade. The walls were papered with crimson flowers on a brick-red ground. Not a map was visible on them from floor to ceiling, from corner to corner. Instead, there were two primitive chromos—one of Daniel in a purple robe, surrounded by a group of amiable mustard-yellow lions; the other of Moses in scarlet, striking a green rock in the presence of four bored Israelites in blue. Between these was hung a memorial-card setting forth the age and virtues of Ellen Elizabeth Corin Jose, deceased; and under the card was a faded photograph of the departed lady in a gilt tin frame.

The musty little room, once the pride of her heart, was now her gaudy cenotaph. As it had been in her life, so it remained, keeping her memory green. Its comic ugliness became impressive, when one thought of it as witnessing to the living influence of a narrow boxful of dust and bones. If its walls were mapless, it was because her wife-like attitude of contemptuous tolerance towards her husband's hobby had ever stiffened into uncompromising opposition at the least hint of his desire to desecrate

the shrine of her respectability with the fruits
of his folly. For the parlour is the Cornish
housewife's fetish, her holy of holies, from
which everything savouring of daily life, of use,
of comfort, of the human, one might almost
say, is sedulously banished. It is in the house,
but not of the house—a sanctuary set apart to
minister to one knows not what vague ideals.
To laugh as it were to ridicule all human
aspiration, all yearnings towards something
outside and above the trivial round of days, all ·
attempts to lift man out of himself.

Fancy would not find it hard to picture the
spirit of the late Mrs Jose as haunting her
parlour yet, guarding it against irreverent
intruders, watching Jennifer with jealous eyes
when on Saturdays she lifted the ornaments
one by one and gave them their weekly dusting, shrilling out inaudible directions for their
rearrangement, and wringing her shadowy
hands in spectral despair when the unconscious
Jennifer flanked the big glass vase with the
'cloamen cats' instead of with the mugs
from Plymouth.

The sentiment of awe for the best room, early
inculcated on all Cornish youth, kept Paul at
the threshold, where, without venturing so

much as the toe of his boot across, he contemplated the inner glories with respectful admiration. Then, turning away, his attention was attracted by the canary, which had suddenly stopped singing when he appeared, and was now sitting on its topmost perch, following his movements with its bright black eyes. With every living creature that crossed his path he was impelled to establish personal relations of a kind; so now he began to make overtures of friendship to the little yellow creature.

'Ah, my 'andsome!' he exclaimed, 'pretty Dick, pretty li'll chap!'—and chirruped and whistled, and stuck an amicable finger through the bars of the cage. The bird fluttered wildly from perch to perch, and beat itself against the bars in an agony of terror. Paul expostulated.

'Don't 'ee get egzited. I edn' goin' to hurt 'ee. How are you so fullish?'

Still the bird dashed from side to side, till two or three feathers fell from its wings. Paul grew angry at his failure to fascinate.

'Bistly auld thing!' he exclaimed. 'Stop that dancin', an' pitch us a tune to wance, or I wring the neck of 'ee!'

It clung to the wires in the farthest corner, panting in terror. For a moment Paul eyed it

with wrathful disgust; then suddenly he burst
into a laugh.

'Gum! what an egzitabble chap I am!' he
cried in tones of immense self-appreciation; and
turned away and stepped out of the open
door.

Across the path, a small wicket gate opened
into a tidy little plot of ground, half orchard,
half garden. Under the wind-tortured dwarf
apple-trees the wallflower grew in bright
patches; in the open parts were rows of
cabbages and humble roots. Through the
apple-branches shone the blue sea, seeming to
slant upwards to meet the blue, downward-
slanting sky.

The gate clicked, and Paul, turning, saw
Jennifer entering from the road. She was
bareheaded, and in her hand she carried a
white pitcher. A morning greeting was
shouted from door to gate, and returned with
gentle gravity at closer quarters.

They entered the house together, and
Jennifer set the jug down on the table.

'Been to fetch the milk for brukfas', aha?'
said Paul, peeping into the jug. 'Looks pure
an' good.' He dipped a finger in. 'Warm
from the cow, ef I d' live! That's your sort

I'm ready fur'n when et's ready for me. Where's your da, Jennifer?'

'Gone over to the cove,' she said. Really her way of looking at a chap—looking right through him, you might say—before answering the simplest question, was most disconcerting.

"'Fore brukfas', eh? He's a bustler, sure 'nough. What's he gone for, I wonder?'

'Da said he'd go an' try to set things straight for 'ee,' said Jennifer.

'Set things straight? How?' asked Paul, quite at sea.

She did not explain.

'Da's took a great fancy ti' 'ee,' she said.

'I can see that,' said Paul complacently, 'an' I hope,' he added insinuatingly, 'his daughter do take arter her da.'

Jennifer frowned.

'Look!' she said with emphasis. 'I'd have 'ee understand I don't wish none o' that kind o' fullishness. I edn' wan o' that sort. An' look!' she continued. 'Da was talkin' ti' 'ee last night, an' he forgot that what's said below the planchin' in this house is heard above en. He was talkin' about me, an' I heard what 'a said. 'Twas shameful. Da do mean well, but he shouldn' say such things.

E

'Twas like a knife in me. An' I'd liv you knaw, wance for all, I don't wish nobody comin' round arter me, nor yet arter da's money.'

Her eyes flashed, and she panted a little.

'Time 'nough to say "no" when you're asked, my dear,' said Paul brutally. Then, at the look of calm disdain in her eyes, an unwonted feeling of shame came over him. Direct apology did not come easily to him, but he laughed frankly, and held out his hand.

'There, my dear—shall be as you d' wish. I waan't plague 'ee. An' shake han's, will 'ee! I'm a stranger in the auld place now, an' I'm kind o' lookin' out for friends. Sim' me you're wan worth gettin'. Friends an' no nonsense, eh?'

She put her hand in his.

'Friends an' no nonsense,' she echoed, with a rare smile. It was impossible for any who had dealings with Paul to feel indifferent to him. The atmosphere above him was electrical. Inevitably it either repelled or attracted.

'Now we're comfortable,' he remarked, as their hands separated. 'Two friends to start

wi'—you an' your da—an' two good wans, 'a
b'lieve. That edn' so bad. My life, though,
I'm rawnish! How 'bout brukfas'? Go see
fur'n, there's a good maid.'

The smile reappeared on her face, perhaps at
the practical use to which he was already
putting their new intimacy, perhaps at the
abrupt descent of his emotions from the heart
to a less poetical region. She went to the
fringle, and stirred the sticks under the kettle.
Paul seated himself comfortably on a chair,
perfectly at home.

'That's a noble li'll room we've got in
there,' he said, indicating the parlour-
mausoleum. 'Full o' stately ornaments.'

Jennifer faced him abruptly.

'I *hate* en!' she exclaimed in low, vehement
tones. ''Tes like a death-chamber to me.
Et do smell o' the grave. 'Tes cauld in there
in the het o' summer-time. I hate en. I'd
block up door an' window ef I had my
will.'

'No! How?' queried Paul, glancing un-
comfortably through the door at the grim
chairs, and cold, gaudy crockery.

'That room hasn' been used for comp'ny,
not sence they ate the cakes an' drank the

wine there at mother's berrin',' said Jennifer.
They that sat last on those chairs were all in
black. They whispered an' shaked their heeds
when they looked 'pon me—a little maid that
dedn' understand, an' dedn' give a thought for
nothin' but the nice cakes an' the sweet wine.
I hate en: the sun do sim to go black out
when et shines through the window of en.
When I go in, I do feel the room full o'
somethin'. I want to look over my shoulder,
an' I don't dare.'

Paul shuddered.

'How?' he whispered. 'Dost mane—?'

'There 'a es,' she hurried on, disregarding
him, 'always the same, year in, year out.
The dust do gather, an' I mus' wipe et off, an'
et do gather agin. Not a cup nor a chair must
I move, or da's vexed. Sim' me, he's afraid o'
mother yet. There 'a es, just as she left en,
an' so 'twill be to the end. 'Tes like a dead
corp' set up among the livin', an' I'm like wan
that's set to brush en an' prink en. I hate
en!'

Her burst of confidence stopped as abruptly
as it had begun. In silence she turned again to
her preparations for the meal.

In Paul's face was the same look of doubtful

fear it had worn the day before at the dis-
astrous omen of the birds.

'Caan't make this out for my life,' he muttered. 'Sim' me, I'll go somewheres else.
This edn' a house to live in.'

He glanced furtively in the direction of the
room, fidgeted on his seat, rose, made two
steps towards the door, faltered, and turned
suddenly to Jennifer.

'Shut the door, will 'ee?' he exclaimed
roughly. 'Caan't think how you can liv en
open.'

Without comment she complied. He drew a
big breath, and some of his uneasiness left him ;
but he remained unwontedly quiet, his eyes
occupied, now with the closed door, now with
the walls and their maps—maps portray our
earth, but their grotesque, lumpish outlines
convey no suggestion of aught earthly ; they
are as anti-terrestrial as a skeleton is anti-
human—now with Jennifer, her strange, calm
face, her gashly-coloured tresses, her noiseless
movements about the room. He had dropped
into queer quarters, sure enough.

The light of the window was momentarily
obstructed by some one passing, and Mr Jose
entered the door. All uncomfortable feeling

was dispelled at the mere sight of the old fellow, with his kindly, ordinary features, his bald head, and his somewhat gross figure—the figure that comes with restful ease after a life of muscular toil.

With a glance of keen inquiry directed on Paul and Jennifer, he sat down and mopped his forehead.

'Well, sonny,' he said to Paul, 'I've been over to cove, an' I found all the world a-talkin' 'bout you.'

'Sure?' exclaimed Paul, hugely delighted.

'Ess. My life, you made a splash last night! 'Tes nothin' but Paul Carah all over the town.'

Paul laughed a laugh of great satisfaction.

'Ess,' continued Mr Jose. 'Such profanin' I never heerd. They were for drivin' 'ee out o' the place double quick. Aw, my nerves, how they did go 'busin' me for takin' you home!'

Paul's face fell.

'The rogues!' he ejaculated. 'I'll liv 'em knaw I edn' to be stanked upon like that.'

'But I stuck up for 'ee,' said Mr Jose, 'an' tauld 'em what I thought o' the case. "Waan't do, naibours," said I; "you'll get Porthvean a bad name. Cornishmen to turn agin a Cornishman like this, en't fitty," said I. "What's the use of sayin' 'wan an' all' ef you don't stick to en?" said I. An' I argued an' argued, an' tauld 'em what a soshabble, well-be'aved chap I'd found you, an' what good comp'ny you were with your yarns an' ballats, an', says I, "The wan that's agin Paul's agin me too." So when they see I'd took you up, they began to talk more sensible. "Arter all," says wan, "the chap's his father's son; an' a man o' sound doctrine was auld Rob Carah." An' another said, "He's been foreign a long time, an' larned ignorance; liv en be for a bit— he'll do very well b'mby." An' auld Reseigh, that keeps the shop, he spoke up for 'ee; an' he's a chap that's looked up to, I can tell 'ee. There edn' many do care to go agin what Reseigh do say. "There's room for plenty ashore," says he, "and there's room for lashin's on the say. How are you so selfish?" says Reseigh. "The more fingers in Porthvean the more money; the more money the more trade and prosperity," says he.'

'An' the more custom for Reseigh's shop,' interposed Jennifer quietly.

'Ess, well, may be,' said her father softly, laughing. 'Reseigh's a smart wan, sure 'nough. Don't 'ee let'n put black 'pon white for 'ee, sonny, or you'll be sorry. There's people have trusted en for a pound an' paid five, an' still owed the pound arter that. So mind what I say. Deal wed'n you must— there edn' nobody else to deal wi'. But don't get into his g'eat black book that he keeps 'pon the counter. 'Tes like the bottomless pit; they that get in don't never get out agin.'

'I edn' no fool,' said Paul testily. His irritation had been growing for some time. He was impatient of advice and assistance alike. The old chap meant well, no doubt; but Paul could fight his own battles; he didn't require to be pled for before Porthvean as if he was a criminal; and he didn't ask for superfluous counsel in matters of men or of money.

'I edn' no fool,' he repeated crossly. 'I don't put my hand under nobody's foot. An' I don't look to be tauld how to be'ave myself in this and that by nobody, auld or young.'

The mild old man looked at him in gentle surprise.

'No offence, soase,' he said, 'I only thought to help 'ee a bit.'

'Then you don't knaw me yet, uncle,' Paul asserted. 'I edn' wan to ask for help. I stand pon my own feet, I do ; an' I look to my own head to save my heels. That's me.'

'No offence,' repeated Mr Jose earnestly.

'None at all, uncle. But trust me to smell a rogue so fur's I can spy en. I haven' lived seven year 'mong Yankees for nothin'. I'm a match for all the rogues in creation, liv alone this li'll town.'

'Brukfas',' said Jennifer; and the magic word was like the noonday sun on the clouds of Paul's irritation.

'Brukfas', aha!' he exclaimed. 'Look out, auld brukfas'; destruction do wait for 'ee, I give 'ee waernin'! Tay, bread, crame an pilcher's—you edn' long for this world. Here's Paul Carah; say your prayers, auld brukfas'!'

'La, what a chap!' murmured his admiring host. '"Say your prayers, auld brukfas'!" There's a laffable bit o' dialogue for 'ee!'

'Aw, that edn' much!' said the modest young man. 'I don't have to think to say a thing like that. My head's alife wi' such queer auld randigals. Tell 'ee, uncle, you shall laff more in a week wi' me than ever you ded in your life before. I'm a rare wan for a joke, I can tell 'ee. *An'* a rare wan for my vittles. Come, draw up.'

CHAPTER V

HE DREAMS

TOWARDS noon Paul was striding down the road from the cove to East Corner, his mind busy reviewing the events and encounters of a long morning in the village. The review was quite satisfactory—how should it be otherwise? They had been a bit stiff at first, 'twas true, but he had been all cream and sugar, and he had yet to meet the man or woman who could resist Paul Carah when he laid himself out to please. A funny yarn to one, a helping hand in the hauling up of another's boat, a boyish escapade together recalled to the memory of a third—'twas as easy as winking. Even Steve Polkinhorne, who had made himself so obnoxious the night before, had sidled up to him and proffered the hand of unity, and invited him to a friendly glass at the *Fisherman's Arms*. He was no little-drop man,

and had declined, of course ; still the offer was
well-meant, and indicated a very proper spirit
of contrition.

Old Reseigh, too, standing at his shop door,
and looking like a nobleman with his big gold
chain looped across his swelling waistcoat, had
beckoned him in and made much of him, feast-
ing him with sugared biscuits and oranges,
dear to the sweet-toothed Cornishman. An
affable, friendly, generous old chap was Reseigh,
whatever Ben Jose might say. What were his
very words at parting ? ' There's some in this
town, Paul, that's set on drivin' 'ee out, so I
hear. But do you stay where you are, an' snap
your fingers at 'em. I'm your friend. Ef so be
things don't prosper wi' 'ee at first, you're
welcome to anythin' in my shop for the askin',
an' pay when you like an' how you like, fish or
cash, to-morrow, or come nex' year.'

'Twas a superfluous offer, of course ; the
picture of Paul and fortune at variance was
comic in its absurdity ; but what trustful generosity ! what neighbourly devotion !

And the rest were equally cordial—particularly those who had sided against him last night.
But it seemed that nobody wanted a partner on
the fishing—all the boats had their proper com-

plement of men. Nor was there a boat for
sale. Jim Boase, maker of jokes (and incident-
ally of boots and shoes), had one lying idle on
the quay—Paul could see it had not been in the
water for a year at least—but as for Jim Boase
parting with that li'll boat, 'twas out of the
question. He loved that li'll boat like as ef
'twas his own cheeld; it had served him faithful for many a year, and had earned its rest.
Besides, it was that rotten, you could stick
your finger through the bottom of en; 'twould
be downright cheating to take money fur'n; he
had too much regard for Paul to allow him to
risk his life in it. Besides, who knows?—he
might want to do a bit o' fishing himself now
and again, or take his family for a cruise of a
summer evening. No; he was perishing to
oblige Paul, but he couldn' part wi' that li'll
boat. The pigs-crow, however, was always at
Paul's service, if his present quarters failed to
suit him.

A queer chap was old Jim Boase, sure enough
—seemed friendly, though his humour was
fatuous in the extreme. Paul was by way of
being a humorist himself, so he could judge.
To crack a joke now and again was very well;
to poke incessant fun at a man—a travelled

man, a man who had a right to expect others
to be ready with the tribute of admiring respect
he always accorded himself—was quite another
matter. The joke of the pig was stale already
at a first repetition; so was the burlesque
humility of accost, the affectation of extreme
deference, the hand at the ear to catch one's
least word, and all the rest of the monkey-
tricks. To take offence at such stuff was beneath one's dignity; one could afford to ignore
it, pending the preparation of a scheme for
paying the joker back in his own coin — a
master-stroke, which should cover him with
such ridicule that he would never have the
heart to jest again.

H'm; so old Ben Jose had not exaggerated
the extent of his fortune; 'twas two hundred
pounds, sure enough, as every soul in Porthvean
knew. And seemingly Paul was not the only
one to whom the old chap had thrown
out hints about his daughter. Most every
young fellow in the place had had the refusal
of her during the past two years. 'Twas a kind
of mania with the old man; that and the maps
were the two weak spots in an otherwise un-
clouded intellect. But Jennifer was likely to go
begging all her life. Porthvean didn't take to

her at all. A strange-looking maid, with her gashly-coloured hair, which even on Sundays she never curled or drew back in the regulation tight bunch behind her head. And a strange behaved one, too — sitting alone in chapel, walking alone on cliff and moor, disdaining the merry gossip and light-hearted love-making of her natural companions, the youths and maids of the village. Some of the older folks shook their heads when her name was mentioned, and dropped obscure hints, declaring that they would not offend Jennifer Jose, not for a thousand pounds. Plum fullishness that was; still, Paul was not sorry that a bond of friendship had been signed between them.

The thing to do now was to bustle and get a boat, and a partner too, if possible; if not, he would start with nothing but his own ten fingers, rather than delay. Not much time before winter; but he couldn't sit idle—Paul Carah wasn't that sort; a reg'lar busker was he. A week to get a boat and tackle, and to rub up his boyhood's knowledge of currents and landmarks; and then—let the conger beware!

At the corner where the road turned its back on the sea to mount inland, he paused and looked out on the expanse of dancing water, gay with foam-flakes and sun-sparkles. There, for two miles south and east and west, lay the town-meadows of Porthvean, pastured by finny flocks. The eyes of Porthvean ever look towards the sea. Hanging on the face of seaward hills, there is scarcely a house in it but commands a prospect of wide waters. For Porthvean men, as for the guillemots and kittiwakes, the shore is but a perching and resting place. If they know the footpaths for a mile inland, and the main roads for a few miles farther, that is all. But the waters they know, as the landsman knows his native town with all its streets and alleys. Every current, rock, shoal and sounding is familiar to them; not a wrinkle, not a fleck of colour on its surface but has its meaning for their eyes. Their lines and nets, like great sensitive hands and feelers, have probed and groped through and through the swaying mass of water to the ocean floor below. The sea's secrets are their daily reading, engraven on their hearts. To a landsman, this is what makes them, and all others who live by the sea, seem in some measure a race apart. The curtaining sea-spell, the atmosphere of dubious mystery that hangs about the tidal shore, invests the fisherman with a certain fabulous air, as of one dealing with esoteric matters, beyond the ken of ordinary folk. The land we know; but what is this ocean, on which we may not walk or build or dig? What familiarity have we with it? And what manner of men are these, who breathe its wonders all their lives? You see them trustingly drop their nets and traps through that flat, translucent floor, and you are inclined to laugh at their credulity —seeking in the unknown for the invisible; they draw them up, and lo, they are filled with an innumerable life, jewelled and resplendent— an unearthly life, whereof the utter strangeness makes you shudder, as it gasps and dies at a breath of the same air which you find so good and vitally sweet.

Paul stood and gazed. Five minutes passed, and still he gazed. He was a true Celt, and deep down below the eager impulsiveness of his character lay an unexplored spring of dreamy imagination, welling up now and again, and drowning the brisk march of purposeful thoughts in a bubbling, many-coloured riot of fancies.

When he stopped, a ghostly grey heron rose from the beach below, and beat a solemn retreat along the coast. A little flock of sander-

F

lings, running swiftly about the wet shore, took alarm, and fled over the water. Loth to seek a new playground, yet afraid to return, they cast about the bay in wide circles, now making for the shore, and then, just as they seemed about to settle, swerving suddenly and hurrying head-long seaward. Now their wings flickered white against the blue water, now they wheeled and vanished, and again they were a vague flitting shadow, of which the eye could scarcely assure itself. A dozen times they circled thus, while Paul watched them and chased a fleeting simile in their track. They were like—like—what were they like, this band of swift white things, which could vanish and reappear at will, but on which a ban seemed set, that they should never rest on dry land again? What, he wondered, was the fate of the spirits of drowned fisher-men? To what disabilities in the world to come might not the loss of Christian burial expose them? What if these were they, or such as they?

The cruel monster of a sea! The treacherous wolves of waves! And here on the shore stood a puny creature who had pledged himself to a life-long battle with them—one man against the mightiest of Nature's forces. Fear was not in him, but he shivered.

There it lay, calmly, swaying, bright hued, a lovely sight. The little waves ran in and fell prone on the sand, clutching at weed and pebble, which they had not strength enough to drag away with them as they slid back. Like children at play they were. Each one fell with a gentle noise of laughter and a flash of foam-white teeth. Was it innocent childish merriment, or was it rather an involuntary revelation of their true character—the snarl, only half playful, of the young cub-wolf?

Dead water it was, no different from the stagnant pool by the wayside. And yet it was alive, alive with that horrible vitality, the vitality of an inanimate thing. Never still. Men were born, moved through life, were laid to rest; but this dead thing never rested. Now and again the wind lashed it, and it rose in factitious fury, and shattered ships and clutched at men, and dragged them down in its cold grasp.

Dead, yes, but teeming with countless life. His fancy dived under the lively waves to the still, twilight depths below. He saw the mullet and guckoo-fish darting hither and thither, swooping, poising, turning in flocks like gay birds. He saw the great armies of herrings and pilchards that come yearly, no one knows whence, and depart, no one knows whither. He saw the cruel sinuous conger, and the ling, the cowards of the sea—so runs the lore of Porthvean—whom the other fish beat and bite and drive from their food—drive from the hooks even, so that they live the life of beggars, sickly and starved in the midst of plenty. He saw the hungry cod, all gaping maw, and the crafty cuttle, grey floating shadows; and the flat-fish, ray and plaice and turbot, small and big, flap-flapping among the ooze; and the lobsters, pacing in black armour, their delicate antennæ ceaselessly waving; and the furtive sidelong scurrying crabs.

There they were; he knew them all, their tricks and their habits; 'twas his wits against theirs for the rest of his life. At the thought the spell was broken; Paul the dreamer gave place to Paul the man of action. He turned sharply and went on his way. You have seen him for a moment in an unexpected light, one, indeed, in which he hardly recognised himself. In his rough analysis of his own character, such moods found no place; they lay too deep down, and came to the surface too rarely. He was puzzled by them—felt half inclined to resent them.

What put such wisht thoughts into his head, he'd like to know. What had made him stand there like a stone, dreaming profitless, uncomfortable dreams? He was a clever chap, though, to think of such things. They made him shiver, but there was a fearful fascination in them for all that. Life spelt emotion for him, and here was a new sensation. He stopped and turned seaward, trying to revive it. But try as he would, 'twas only the commonplace old sea, the waves were the familiar waves at their weary tumbling work, the sanderlings only suggested a gun and a spit. With a grunt of annoyance he resumed his way.

CHAPTER VI

HE FINDS A PARTNER

HALF-WAY between the gate and the door, Paul's steps were arrested by a sound within the house—an outburst of hoarse chuckling laughter, alternating in a curious way between extreme gruffness and excessive shrillness. There was something bizarre in the sound —something only half human, with a reminiscence in its timbre of the voices of beasts. Paul caught a vague memory on the wing, but failed to identify it. He strode quickly on, and entered the kitchen.

Jennifer was sitting by the window, knitting. Directly facing her, on a chair planted in the centre of the room, sat the figure of a man, with his back to Paul. Just as Paul entered Jennifer raised her eyes and smiled, and again the hoarse chuckle burst with startling abruptness from the lips of the man in the chair.

Then Jennifer saw Paul, and reading this in her look, the man faced round, and fixed Paul with a pair of glittering, steadfast eyes—the eyes of a wild creature. They were deep-set under bushy, far-jutting eyebrows, over which a low, narrow forehead sloped up and back to a bald cranium. The nose was snub and wide-spreading; the jaws, covered with a thick grizzled beard, protruded enormously. The arms were ape-like in their length; the backs of the wrists were black with hair. One looked instinctively for a tail.

'You mind Dummy?' said Jennifer.

'To be sure I do,' cried Paul. 'An' Dummy minds me, I'll be bound. Many's the game I've played en—eh, old chap?'

The glittering eyes were still fastened on him, and the forehead was contracted with the wrinkles of deep thought. Suddenly they cleared away; the man jumped to his feet, and began to pace up and down the room at a furious rate, his head bent forward, his arms swinging wildly.

Paul burst into laughter.

'You've hit en!' he exclaimed. 'That's me—me to the life! 'Tes a pity Dummy's deef and dumb; sim' me he might make a

fortune play - actin'.   Edn' nobody he caan't
take off, 'a b'lieve.   Come, shake han's, auld
chap.'

At the sight of the proffered hand, Dummy
pulled up sharply.   The wrinkles swarmed on
his forehead again, his hands darted behind
his back, his head began to shake with such
velocity that its outline was blurred, like that
of a revolving wheel, and from his lips burst
forth a fierce inarticulate chatter, like an en-
raged monkey's.

Paul's hand dropped.

'Even Dummy waan't shake han's!' he
cried despondently.   'How don't 'ee shake
han's, Dummy?'

Dummy's eyes swept round the kitchen.
He darted to a shelf and seized the teapot.
He held it up and tapped it vehemently.   He
set it down on the floor, retired a pace, and
imitated the action of one pelting it with stones.
And again the head wagged with incredible
swiftness, and again and again the stuttering
torrent burst from his lips.

Paul saw light.

'My life!' he exclaimed, 'to think of his
mindin' *that* all these years!   You d' knaw,'
he explained to Jennifer, 'how, summer-time,

Dummy don't trouble to light a fire for his tay, but takes the taypot round to a naibour to get'n filled with hot water. Well, one day us lads saw Dummy goin' along, carryin' his taypot, an' we started teasin' him. An' I picked up a bully an' aimed et at the taypot. Dummy thought I was aimin' at him, so he set the taypot down an' sarched for a bully to aim back. An' then I heaved another bully, an' hit the taypot, sure 'nough—smashed en all to jowds. Dummy's back was turned ; 'a dedn' see the smash, an' course, bein' deef, 'a dedn' hear en. We runned away, an' Dummy turned round to pick up his taypot, an'—well, you never saw such ·a rage in all your life. Out comes his knife, an' arter us he goes. 'Twas a mercy he dedn' catch us, or there'd ha' been murder, sure 'nough. Vicious as a monkey, Dummy is. Look at en now ! '

Dummy had shambled off to the door ; and there he stood, half averted, growling and talking to himself, as it were, with subdued gesticulations. Jennifer showed some indignation.

'' 'Tes a shame,' she said, ' the way you d' all be'ave to en. No wonder he's a bit teasy when you plague en so, the poor afflicted creature !'

She raised her hand above her head, and Dummy turned and came to her, like a dog to the whistle. With a tender sadness in her eyes, she patted his shoulder, soothing him.

'Dummy an' me, we're swettards,' she said. 'He was courtin' me when you came in. An' some day, when he's arned enough, he'll come sailin' into the bay 'pon a g'eat four-mast steamer—nothin' but four masts 'ull do fur'n, he's that fond o' me—an' he'll carr' me off to get married. An' we're goin' to live up to squire's house, an' have crame every day, an' the biggest, grandest taypot in Porthvean. So, you see, they that look to be friends wi' me mus' be friends wi' Dummy too.'

'That's so, aha?' said Paul, highly amused. 'Well, I'm ready. Courtin' of 'ee, is 'a? That's grand. An' a four-master to carr' 'ee off in? There's a laffable notion for 'ee. Squire's house, too? Aw, my life!'

Laughing heartily, he flung himself into a chair and spread his long legs abroad. The bright eyes turned suspiciously on him, and

a low growl issued from the speechless lips.
Paul sat up.

'What's the matter now?' he asked.

'Dummy thinks you're laffin' upon 'm,'
said Jennifer. 'He don't like to be made
fun of.'

'Right!' said Paul, all complaisance, and
composed his features to an expression of
intense melancholy. 'How's that?'

But Dummy was not appeased. The growls
increased in volume; the hands started from
the pockets and waved about with profuse
gesture.

'There's somethin' else,' said Jennifer,
studying the movement of the hands. She
lifted her arm again. Dummy's eyes went
swiftly to her face. She raised her brows in
question. Dummy's arms whirled with increased velocity; his hands pointed in quick
succession to Paul, to Jennifer, to himself.
A faint blush appeared on Jennifer's cheek.

'Dummy do want to knaw what you're
doin' here,' she explained. 'He edn' used to
seein' young chaps makin' themselves at home
here. Sim' me'—she hesitated, and the blush
grew deeper—'sim' me, he's jealous.'

Paul grinned complacently, and twirled the

ends of his moustache. Jealous, aha? Jennifer
was nothing to him, but it was exceedingly
flattering to find that his mere presence in her
company proved disturbing to another man's
peace of mind, even if that other were only
Dummy. And that blush, too: it hadn't
escaped him. These women! they may talk
fine stuff and pretend to hold aloof, but one
knows them. A blush, a gesture, and they
stand revealed, head bowed and heart bared
to the conqueror.

What were they up to now, swaying their
hands and rolling their eyes? He had lost
the hang of this dummy-talk in all these years.
His foot tapped impatiently on the floor. His
ignorance thrust him aside from the central
position which was his by right. The presence
of the uncomprehended irritated him intensely.

Jennifer turned to him.

''Tes all right now,' she said. 'Dummy
do knaw all about :'ee, an' he's willin' to be
friendly. Edn' no real malice in Dummy.'

'Brave an' kind of en, I'm sure,' said Paul
sulkily; 'an' thank'ee for interferin'. But I
don't wish no truck wi' monkeys.'

She looked at him, and turned away. A
most annoying sense of shame came over him.

What was coming to him, that a contemptuous look from a maid—and a homely maid at that—should cause him humiliation?

But there was Dummy standing over him, his hand extended, his ugly face stretched into a comic grin that no mortal with a sense of humour could resist. Laughing uproariously, Paul leapt to his feet and slapped Dummy vigorously on the shoulder. Dummy laughed back, and returned the friendly · blow with interest.

'That's right!' said Jennifer, smiling approval.

Paul glowed with magnanimous feeling.

'Edn' a bad sort, Dummy edn',' he said patronisingly.

Jennifer warmed in extolment of her favourite.

'There edn' a better-hearted chap in Porthvean,' she declared, 'ef you take en the right way. Poor chap; he's sensible too — you caan't think how sensible 'a es. Give him a newspaper, an' he'll skrink up his brows an' jabber over en, as ef he was readin'. An' ef 'tes upside down, he'll turn et round the right way. An' there edn' a smarter hand at makin' crab-pots anywhere. He's slow, but he finishes 'em· up beautiful—that neat an' strong! An' for fishin', there edn' nobody to come up to him. He knows where they resort, an' all their tricks an' ways, so well as ef he'd lived under the water. Over to cove they do say he can smell the fish. But, sim' me, 'tes because Dummy edn' like other men. I d' often think he edn' azackly human, nor he edn' azackly a dumb brute, but somethin' between, like-a-thing. He's sensible, but 'a edn' quite the sense of a man—more like the sense of a dog or a sea-gull. They do see things we don't get a notion of; an' so for Dummy. An' I do often wonder what like his thoughts are. We do think in words, sim' me; but Dummy don't know wan word from another, no more 'n a cat. An' I do wonder what the world must be like to en—all movin', movin', wi' never a sound; an' when he do shut his eyes, there's nothin'.'

She was not addressing Paul now; her eyes were fixed dreamily on the other, and she was thinking aloud to herself. Neither was Paul heeding her latterly; a new and brilliant idea was buzzing about his brain.

Look!' he exclaimed suddenly. 'Whose boat do Dummy go 'pon?'

Sometimes wan, sometimes another,' said

Jennifer. 'They're always glad to get en,
but he don't stay long wi' none. They don't
know how to trate en ; they tease him an' vex
him, an' off 'a goes in a tantrum. Steve
Polkinhorne was the last he went wi', but Steve
thought to cheat en out of his share in the fish.
Dummy was sharper than Steve thought, for
he found en out to wance, an' knocked en
down 'pon quay-head an' jumped upon 'm, till
they had to pull him off.'

'Brayvo Dummy !' cried Paul. 'Dummy's
the chap for me ! He's my sort. Look ! I've a
mind to do en a good turn. How ef him an'
me should go partners 'pon the fishery ? ' Edn'
that a smart notion, aha ? Gum ! I'll make
Dummy's fortune fur'n before he do know
where he is. An' then, hoorah for the four-
master, an' squire's house, an' the crame, an'
the taypot ! Ha-ha ! Poor chap ! But I'll be
tender wed'n—tender as a mother with her
cheeld.'

Jennifer seemed to think the notion a feasible
one.

' 'Twill be a good thing for you,' she said, ' ef
you can get en to agree.'

'For me ? ' Paul corrected her. 'For him
you d' mane, s'pose.'

She smiled a little, but did not dispute the point.

'I'll ask him,' she said.

'Wait a bit,' Paul exclaimed. 'I'll do et myself. Mus' get inside this dummy-talk some time, s'pose. May as well fit an' begin now. You watch now, an' see how smart I can do et.'

He raised his arm, as he had seen Jennifer do, and Dummy faced round at attention.

Paul pointed a finger at his own chest, then at Dummy's. He slapped his right hand down into his left, and shook it vigorously.

'We're goin' partners, that do mane,' he explained to Jennifer.

He pointed again to himself, thrust his arms forward with fists clenched side by side, and drew the fists back to his chest. Repeating this action two or three times, he then pointed to Dummy, and hauled an imaginary rope downwards, hand over hand.

'On a boat, you d' see, rowin' an' sailin',' he said.

He leaned over the back of a chair, and hauled another imaginary rope upwards.

'Fishin',' he remarked.

He went down on all fours and scuttled sideways across the room.

'Crabbin',' he observed.

He thrust his hand into his pocket, drew it out tightly clenched, and with the other hand distributed from it two heaps of nothingness on to the table. One heap he feigned to pick up and return to his pocket; and he beckoned Dummy to approach and take the other.

'Goin' shares,' he said.

Dummy, who had followed Paul's essay in the pantomimic art with grave attention, now raised his eyes inquiringly to Jennifer. She nodded, and Dummy stepped up to the table and made as if to gather up the invisible coins.

''Tes a bargain!' cried Jennifer, and clapped her hands.

Paul wiped his brow.

'That was clever, wadn' et?' he said. 'Sim' me, this dummy-talk's fine fun. Easy 'nough, ef you use your brain, an' that's what I do like. *An'* your arms! Must be a sweaty business, summer-time! Fine times we'll have, aha, auld chap?' This to Dummy, who was nodding and grinning and making little chuckling noises.

'Look at en! Plaised as Punch, 'a es!

G

We're a pair! *We*'ll liv 'em knaw; *we*'ll
make 'em sit up an' scratch their chins! Edn'
'a just the chap I do want for my partner? For
look—I'm schemin' all the while, an' I don't
wish nobody to knaw my plans; but my natur'
's that open, I'm fo'ced to tell 'em to somebody,
or burst. An' here I've got a partner I can
talk to all day, an' tell all my secrets, an' he nor
nobody else waan't be none the wiser. I couldn'
ha' found a more suitable chap, not ef I picked
the world over.'

He surveyed Dummy with the eager proprie-
tory delight of a child with a new play-
thing.

'But that's me,' he continued. 'I d' allers
hit upon what I do want. Luck, you say; but
no, 'a edn' luck. I don't believe in luck. Luck's
for fools an' sluggards. Look! The river o'
life, they do say. We're standin' in et, up to
our middles; an' down the stream comes fortune an' misery, riches an' rags—like driftwood;
an' we're snatchin' an' grabbin' at 'em as they
pass. The sluggard do wait fur'n to come
plop agin his chest, an' the fool do grab pro-
misc'us; but the smart man keeps his han's
ready an' his eyes up-stream, an' everythin' that
comes by, he takes the measure of en. Ef 'tes

no account, he pushes et away ; ef 'tes good—
splash ! snatch !—he's got en !'

By way of illustration, he leaped upon
Dummy and clutched his shoulder, sending him
back, jabbering in angry alarm, to the remotest
corner of the room.

'Ha-ha !' roared Paul. 'Good as a play,
edn' 'a ? Don't get egzited, auld chap. 'Tes
only my fun—Paul Carah's fun !'

'That's what Dummy don't understand,'
said Jennifer. 'You med as well joke with a
cow as with Dummy.'

'Poor chap !' said Paul, staring at him with
unfeigned pity. It was sad to think that his
new partner was congenitally incapable of ap-
preciating some of his best qualities.

CHAPTER VII

HE BUYS A BOAT

IF the grass thought to grow under Paul's feet, the grass was ill-advised. Early next morning he was off, with a pasty in each pocket, on a tramp along the coast in search of a boat wanting an owner. Late at night he returned, tired, hungry, and jubilant, his pockets lighter by the weight of the pasties and of half his little store of gold. Trying southward at first, he had drawn blank at Portrewan and Lanharry. Then, nothing daunted, he turned back, passing Porthvean again, and making for Porthellick. Here his panting, perspiring luck caught him up. He reached Porthellick at the psychological moment, just two days after the receipt of William John Harvey's letter. William John, a feckless, luckless fellow, had lately left his birthplace to try his fortune in London town, and Porthellick had shaken its head, having long since identified London with Bunyan's City of Destruction. But after a month of silence William John had written to his sweetheart—and what was this? A pound a week, regular as clockwork, just for tying up parcels! Dainty meals of sausages and onions smoking in shop windows, sending forth their alluring smell through the streets from dawn to midnight! Wondrous sights— trains that burrowed underground, mighty bridges that split in half and folded up at the touch of a lever! Could such things be?

An adventurous fever seized Porthellick. Within twenty-four hours Michael Harvey had packed and set off to join his brother. Several other young men were only waiting to wind up their affairs before following his example; and others again hesitated, the hand of hereditary caution plucking at the coat-tails of enthusiasm. Among these was Will Oliver, whose meditated flight into the unknown was further hampered by a brand-new boat and a brand-new wife. To him enter Paul, voluble, persuasive, jingling the gold in his pockets, a living witness to the advantages, material and moral, of foreign travel. The wife? The wife could stay behind for a bit. The boat? Paul would take the

boat off his hands there and then, and pay for
it in solid cash. Fifteen pounds, now! A poor
sum in Porthellick—the moss would be growing
on it before one had a chance to turn it over.
But fifteen pounds in London, with a brave
Cornishman to back it up; la! in a week 'twould
swell and burst the brave Cornishman's pocket!

Will Oliver succumbed; the money was
transferred on the spot; and in twelve hours
after Paul's departure Mr Jose and Jennifer
were listening to his pæan of self-gratulation.

'Smartest li'll boat 'pon the fishery—don't
knaw of a nobler li'll boat anywheres—a reg'lar
picture! Cost thirty pound; hasn' been in the
water a dozen times, an' I get'n for fifteen,
gear and all complete. That's my way. But
you should ha' heard me argufyin' wi' the
chap! *I* managed en! Says he—"'Tes a
ticklish business, goin' foreign; my heart do
sink to think upon et." Says I—" Look at me,
soase, an' take heart. Look at me," says I,
"look at my chest an' my pocket," says I,
slappin' first the wan an' then the other. " That's
foreign travel," says I. " Aw well," he say,
" I'll ax the missus an' see what she do say."
Well, thinks I, ef he do, fare-'ee-well, smart
li'll boat. I d' knaw the women. So I say to

'n—"Have 'ee the sperit of a man in 'ee? Art wan o' they that do go to their wives, whip in one hand an' money-bag in the other, an' say— ''Ere, take these an' rule over me?'" Shame upon 'ee for a man!" I said to en. "Go to your wife, an' whether she say yes or whether she say no, *you* waan't see much o' these fifteen bright pounds," I said, haulin' out a handful. You should ha' seen the eyes of en gog-glin'! "Gie me the money!" he say, "the boat's yourn!" An' mine 'a es, an' the bargain too. 'Twas smart, but I don't take no credit for gettin' round a simple chap like he. Sim' me, *he* waan't make much of a splash in London town. Chaps like he should stay at home, though I wadn' a-goin' to tell en so. An' home he'll be 'fore long, with empty pockets, sure 'nough.'

'Poor chap!' said Jennifer.

'Ha! ha! Poor chap!' echoed Paul.

'An' you sent him,' said Jennifer, 'or as good as sent him—parted him from his wife, an' cheated him over his boat, an' druv him to ruin, maybe! Aw, you're a smart chap, Paul Carah!'

'How?' exclaimed Paul, amazed, as he well might be, at the lurid light thus suddenly

cast on his transactions. 'How?' he repeated, pricked by wrath and by another
emotion which he would not recognise.
'Pouf!' he cried, ''tes the way o' business.
Edn' in a woman to understand business.'

''Tes in a woman to understand roguery,'
said Jennifer warmly.

Her anxious parent interposed with as near
an approach to severity as he could achieve.

'What are 'ee a-tellin' of, Jennifer? Roguery?
I wonder at 'ee. Don't talk like that—'a edn'
fitty 'tall. What's Paul done? Druv a good
bargain. Ef that's roguery we're all rogues
together, your auld da an' all. Don't go for to
call your auld da a rogue!'

Paul joined in with grave reproof.

'Ess, I wonder at 'ee, Jennifer. 'Twas all
honest an' fair, wadn' 'a? All the world do
knaw what a bargain is—two honest men tryin'
to cheat aich other. There's honest cheatin'
an' there's roguish cheatin'. 'Sides,' he added,
weakly sliding into a shaky morass of self-
justification, 'I guv the chap 'most what his
boat was worth; he couldn' look for more,
sellin' in such a hurry. An' I've no doubt he'll
do very well up to London; he's just as like to
as not. Anyways, he was main set on goin'

—don't s'pose anythin' I said could stop him.'

Jennifer's shoulder was towards him, and he desisted. This slip of a maid had an unpleasant power of making one uncomfortable, of driving a mind conscious of rectitude to paltry, unnecessary shifts and evasions. He had it in him to dislike her furiously.

Mr Jose fidgeted uneasily, feeling vaguely that his paragon had not distinguished himself, conscious of having inwardly applauded what Jennifer had condemned. There was thunder in the air. A tactful change of subject might divert it.

'What's the name o' the little boat?' he asked.

'*Swiftsure*,' said Paul, shortly.

'An' a good name too. An' when do 'ee bring her round here-along?'

Paul's manner changed.

'Don't knaw azackly,' he said mysteriously. 'I've got somethin' else to see for first. There's a scheme plummin' in my head. Look, don't say nothin' over to cove 'bout the boat, nor yet 'bout Dummy. I've got a plan to surprise 'em. I'll open their eyes! I'll make them stare!'

'How?' asked Jennifer, relaxing. She was not altogether free from what is fabled to be the chief failing of her sex.

Paul took his little revenge.

I waan't tell 'ee yet. 'Tes a brave plan, though,' he said, and ostentatiously changed the subject.

Next morning he disappeared, returning in the evening with a brown-paper parcel and a flow of talk about Henliston market. The parcel was not opened or referred to. Jennifer respected the sanctity of the carefully tied knots, but when Paul was absent, she had the curiosity to prod and weigh. It felt like calico, which set her wondering.

The following day Dummy came round early, and he and Paul went off together, after Paul had called Mr Jose and Jennifer aside and told them to go down upon quay-head about four o'clock, if they wanted to see some fun.

Late that afternoon Bob Rowe, hanging a trammel over the quay wall to dry, saw a boat rounding the point which limits Porthvean's view of the coast to the north-east. It was too far away to distinguish details, but Bob noticed something peculiar about its appearance, and

called the other men to come and look. They
could make nothing of it either. A messenger
was despatched to the coastguard station for a
telescope. He returned with two coastguardsmen and a little crowd of men and women.
Attracted by the stir, others hurried down, till
there was quite a mob on the quay.

The coastguardsman who held the telescope
rested it on the wall and took a long look.

'Well? What is 'a?' was queried.

'My life!' murmured the coastguardsman, his
eye glued to the glass. 'My dear life! Well!
well!'

'What?' cried the impatient crowd.
'Spake up an' tell us.'

''Tes a fishin' boat,' said the man slowly.
'Porthellick boat, 'a b'lieve. An' there's flags
on it.'

'Flags? Porthellick boat wi' flags?'

'Flags on the mainmast, flags on the mizen,
flags in the bow, flags at the starn, an' a lot of
teeny flags all up the riggin'?'

'*What* are 'ee a-tellin' of?' cried the
astonished multitude with one voice.

'See else,' said the coastguardsman, prof-
fering the telescope. It was seized by half-
a-dozen eager hands. A brief struggle, and

Jim Boase was the victor. There was a breathless silence while he adjusted the focus.

''Tes Will Oliver's boat, the *Swiftsure*,' he proclaimed. ' I knaw her by the new sails.'

' Will Oliver ? ' said one. ' Has his wife druv him mazed already ? '

The laughter was checked as Jim held up a hand.

Two men in her,' he said, ' an' nuther wan's Will.'

' Who then ? '

Wait a bit. I caan't make 'em out yet.'

Favoured by the wind, the strange boat was rapidly approaching, its fantastic adornments now visible to every eye. Wondering conjectures were tossed from lip to lip. Ben Jose on the outskirts winked and chuckled to himself.

Suddenly a yell of mingled surprise and laughter burst from Jim Boase.

' Yah-ha-ha ! Now I see 'en ! Ess—'tes he agin, sure 'nough ! '

' Who ? Who, thou bussa ? '

' An', my nerves, ef the other chap edn'— oh-ho-ho ! '

They were ready to massacre him.

' *Who ?* Stop grizzlin', an' tell us who ! '

'Paul!' he gasped. 'The g'eat Paul
Carah comin' in glory an' triumph, an' steered
by Dummy hisself!'

Their amazement was too great for laughter.

'What a chap!' was murmured. 'What
a chap, to be sure! All they flags! Who
ever heerd tell o' such a thing? An' Dummy,
an' Will Oliver's new boat! What a chap!'

All eyes were fixed on the approaching craft.
Soon they could discern the occupants. 'Twas
Paul, sure enough; and see! he was waving
a flag in each hand. And now he was hailing
them. Some one raised a cheer, and the
majority took it up, half in joke, half in earnest.
Nearer came the boat. Deftly steered by the
beaming Dummy, it shaved the pier-head and
brought up alongside, all standing.

Up clambered Paul, and by inveterate habit
began shaking hands all round.

'What d'ye think o' that, aha?' he exclaimed. 'Looks gay, don't 'a? Thought
I'd give 'ee all a surprise. Dedn' knaw I'd
got a boat, ded 'ee? *An'* a partner! Hup,
Dummy! step up an' show yourself! Smart
li'll boat, edn' 'a? An' a rare wan to go, I can
tell 'ee. Hooraw! Shake han's, naibours all!'

He was dancing with excitement. 'Twas

the hour of his glory, eclipsing, utterly blotting out, as he had planned it should, the unpleasant memory of his first reception. A dramatic situation, a cloud of flying bunting, a cheering crowd—what more could the heart of man desire, what higher pinnacle attain to? For what but this does the world strive and struggle, statesmen, warriors and all?

'Aw, Paul, Paul!' exclaimed Jim Boase in mock anguish. 'How dedn' 'ee give us a hint, so's we could 'a had St Kerne brass band down?'

The crowd lined the edge of the quay, unrestrainedly admiring the *Swiftsure* in its gay attire. Cornish folk are as easily pleased as children of a smaller growth, and as grateful and well-disposed to any that will afford them entertainment. Paul's popularity was high at that moment. True, there was a fringe of scowling faces on the outskirts, and Steve Polkinhorne, slightly the worse for drink, was muttering imprecations on the conceit and insolence of some folk, making a maygame of their betters with their play-acting, flag-flying nonsense. But Steve and his followers were in a miserable minority. Most cast aside prejudice, and frankly admitted that a chap who could plan and execute such a scheme as this for their entertainment, was a chap to be encouraged, a genuine acquisition.

And what was this? Old Reseigh himself taking the trouble to walk down the quay, condescending to shake Paul by the hand, and warmly congratulating him!

'Very smart an' pretty,' quoth he, his little eyes wandering from the boat to Paul, and from Paul to Dummy. 'A grand notion, sure 'nough, an' we do take et kind of 'ee to make such a brave show for us to see. An' you've got a boat an' a partner already, spite o' the rogues that looked to hender 'ee. You're a smart chap, an' a bustler, that's plain. I'll keep my eye upon 'ee; you should do very well ef you've a mind to. An' look—you'll be wantin' gear. There's everythin' in my li'll shop—nets, lines, hooks. Come an' choose when you like, an' you needn' bring no money.'

'That your game, uncle?' exclaimed Paul, slapping the great man on the shoulder in a familiar way which made those around shudder and fearfully admire. 'No debts for me. What I take I pay for; that's me!'

'You're right,' said Reseigh with a sidelong glance. 'You're my sort, I can see—a man o' business. I only said that to show 'ee where to look for help when you want et. I'm your friend, mind that. Steve Polkinhorne, come along o' me. I want you.'

The crowd parted respectfully as old Reseigh waddled off with Steve skulking behind him. As soon as the two were at a safe distance, nods and winks of deep import were exchanged. The nature of the bond between them was known, but it was not a thing to talk of aloud with safety, especially when coastguardsmen were about.

Reseigh gone, the suspended interest in Paul and his boat revived. They crowded round, questioning and admiring. Paul was in his element, and he shone—joking, yarning, boasting, till at last he grew too hoarse for intelligible speech, and took Ben Jose's arm and walked off, the happiest man in Cornwall that day.

'I've guv 'em somethin' to talk about, aha, uncle?' he said exultingly. 'I tauld 'ee you all wanted wakin' up, an' I'm the man to do et. I edn' wan to be overlooked! Grand, wadn' et? The eyes of all Porthvean upon me, 'a b'lieve. 'Tes a pity Jennifer dedn' come. How dedn' she?'

Ben Jose hesitated.

'Well, she dedn' wish,' he said apologetically. 'She guv a guess o' what was up, an' she don't sim to set no store by such things. A queeat maid, you d' knaw. She edn' wan for show an' fuss an' mummery.'

'S'pose not,' said Paul in tones of vexation; and suddenly he dropped into a silence.

CHAPTER VIII

HE MAKES AN ENEMY

FAINT colours were beginning to mantle in the grey face of the dawn, when the *Swiftsure*, with Paul and Dummy on board, slipped out of the arms of the sleeping quay, and turned southward along the coast. In the chill morning air Dummy yawned and shivered, only half awake. Paul was fresh and alert, warm with the glow of enterprise. Early as it was, he had already spent some busy hours at the cuttling grounds, getting bait. For after a week of unremitting toil everything was ready, the ropes tarred, the nets barked, the hooks fitted to spiller and boulter, and now at last he sat in his own boat with his trusty partner by his side, speeding on his way to make the first cast in his new and hopeful venture. Dummy steered, while Paul cut up the cuttle ready for the hooks. Past Carn Mellyn they

went, and out towards Penluce, tacking to and
fro in the teeth of the breeze : for 'tis the rule
to beat up against the weather when going out,
so as to ensure a fair run home if the wind
should rise. Half - way to Penluce, Dummy
steered out to sea. Hitherto he had remained
quietly intent on the guidance of the boat ; but
now, as they left the land behind, he began
to chatter to himself, and his eyes wandered
restlessly about, now peering over the side
of the boat into the water, now searching the
hills behind for landmarks, now comprehensively sweeping from sea to sky and back
again, reading an open book, as it seemed,
and pondering on its sentences. Now he
laughed, and now he frowned and chattered
angrily. Sometimes he let the tiller go for a
moment, and wove excited gestures on the air,
as if arguing with himself. Once or twice
he leaned over as he sat, scooped up a little
water in the palm of his hand, and tasted it.
His excitement infected Paul, who, from
watching him in curious silence, broke out
into the little inarticulate cries with which a
sportsman encourages his dog.

Still they went on, until they were about a
mile from shore. The sun was up a hand's

breadth from the horizon, and the boat danced on the verge of a broad track of pale fire. Shags flew low over the water and squattered down in spurts of diamond spray. The gulls were shouting overhead, and Paul in sheer high spirits shouted back.

On they went. The shags were swimming all round them. Every moment one would dive, leaping right out of the water and describing a curve in the air with its black snaky body before disappearing below. One appeared suddenly right under the boat's quarter with a bar of living silver in its beak. Paul shouted a greeting, as to a comrade.

'Good luck ti' 'ee, soase! How's the fishin' hereabouts?'

Just as he spoke, Dummy, taking the hint, as Paul opined, from the bird, relinquished the tiller, cast loose the main sheet, and made signs for Paul to help him lower the sails.

'We're there, aha?' cried Paul, clutching and tugging at the ropes in a frenzy of excitement. 'Bustle, brave boys! Down with her! Yo-o-o-hup! That's your sort! Smart's the word!'

The sails down, they set about preparing

the tackle. First Dummy adjusted the lines by which the boulter was to hang from the floats. Then he started baiting the hooks, treating each one with a deliberate carefulness, which set Paul's highly strung nerves a-fidget. He wanted to help, but Dummy snatched the line from his hands with an angry chatter. He knew his business, his heart was in it, and he brooked no interference from novices. Paul tried to argue, but argument by gesture is hopeless work, and Dummy's eyes were too busy to attend. Paul began to realise that between two men, one with all his five senses, and the other with only three, the advantage is not always with the better-equipped. When one like Dummy wished to go on his own way, he had only to blink his eyes or turn his back, and he was impermeable to all external influence save actual force. The glib tongue on which Paul set such reliance was of no service here.

With another man Paul would have fired up at being pushed into the background on board his own boat; but Dummy to him was one huge joke. He laughed and acquiesced, content to stand by Dummy's side and pay out the boulter section by section, thrilling with the hunter's joy to see it sink down and down into the dim underworld where the invisible quarry lurked, picturing the moment when it would next come to light, strung from end to end with flapping, tugging, wriggling creatures.

The last hook was baited, the last float flopped into the water. The sails were hoisted again, and the *Swiftsure* danced homeward, a thing of springing, stressful life, a swift, brown-winged bird. The old similes must suffice.

Paul had the tiller now, and his heart overflowed with the joy of life, and that sense of power and mastery which is only known in its completeness to two—the steersman in a fair breeze and the musician playing on a great organ. He sang, he laughed, he addressed his boat in terms of extravagant endearment, as a lover his mistress. He talked and joked with Dummy, as a man will talk and joke with his dog, in a spirit of make-believe that the creature understands. And as the dog wags a sociable and courteous tail, so Dummy grinned and gabbled back.

Steve Polkinhorne, lounging on the quay, watching the approach of the boat and revolv-

ing dark thoughts, was treated to a faded
music-hall song, yelled with all the force of
Paul's lungs. He had hated and feared the
insolent, overbearing fellow from the first.
To see him approaching thus, as it were in
triumphal progress, with the wind of fortune
at his back and a song of jubilee on his lips,
affected him intolerably. As Paul and Dummy,
having made fast, clambered up on to the quay,
he advanced towards them, and accosted Paul
with a nasty grin.

'Welcome home agin, my lord!' he snig-
gered.

'Aha, Steve, my boy! fine fishin' weather,'
said Paul genially, for he was at peace with
all the world just then. But he had no time to
spare for a chat with idle fellows. With a wave
of his hand he swung off up the quay. Steve,
ready to construe anything from Paul into an
insult, snarled an ugly word under his breath,
stepped up to the edge of the quay, and deliber-
ately spat into the boat below. But though
Paul was off, Dummy was close at hand, and
the boat Dummy sailed on was as sacred to
him as his ancestral bones to the bland
Celestial. With a shriek of rage he leapt on
Steve, and began pounding him. Steve howled

murder, and Paul, hurrying back, was only just
in time to save him from being toppled over into
the water by his infuriated antagonist. He
pushed his long arms between the two, and
with a vigorous thrust sent them staggering
back in contrary directions.

'Ef that jabberin' monkey lays a hand 'pon
me agin,' gasped Steve, 'I'll put a knife into
'm.'

''Ere, what's all this about?' exclaimed
Paul.

'Nothin',' muttered Steve. 'He jumped
'pon me when my back was turned. He ought
to be shut up ; he's as vicious as a fox.'

'How's this, Dummy?' asked Paul.
Dummy explained in vigorous pantomime.
Paul's face darkened.

'Oh, you did, did you?' he blazed out.
'Well, do that agin, or the likes of et, or go
to touch my partner or profane agin him, an'
you'll get the noblest hidin' you ever had in
your life. Monkey, sayst? I liv you knaw
he's a better man than any drunken, cheatin'
rogue 'mong *your* lot. Be off wi' 'ee, before I
smash 'ee. The likes o' you edn' fit for humans
to consort wi'. An' we don't have no transactions arter this, mind that.'

Steve slunk off, swearing abominably. At the end of the quay he turned.

'Yah!' he yelled. 'Yah, thou bussa! I'll be even wi' 'ee yet, thou hollerin' faggot! I give 'ee fair warnin', so look out!'

'Thank 'ee, thank 'ee!' laughed Paul. 'But you needn' ha' troubled. When I see a snake, I don't need to hear his rattle 'fore I stank upon 'm. Do your worst, I'm ready.'

Later on, Jennifer was favoured with a highly-coloured version of the whole occurrence; and she expressed her satisfaction in terms of warm approval—the first she had accorded him. If she smiled a little when he spoke in stern reprobation of the insulting epithet Steve had applied to Dummy, yet her smile was kindly. She was beginning to understand Paul, and to see that to understand him was to be disposed to excuse the flamboyant eccentricities which at first had repelled her. If nothing else, then his prompt championship of her favourite inclined her to tolerance.

So, with fortune and (by what he would consider a poetic licence) beauty smiling on our hero, this chapter comes to a fine-weather close.

CHAPTER IX

HE GOES FISHING

ON Monday night the wind got up, and all through Tuesday and Wednesday it rained and blew a regular twister. Paul's whole thoughts were concentrated on the slender cord that swayed and stretched out there in mid-sea, carrying his hopes and fortune. He fretted and fumed outrageously at the delay the weather was causing. He could lay no claim to the fisherman's chief and most necessary virtue, the steady, uncomplaining patience which sits about our coasts, and whittles its stick when winds are high. He found fault with his food; he was testy and irritable with Jennifer; and when the lamp was lit and Mr Jose lugged down his mapping tackle and set to work on Scotland, which is no light job, with its superfluously intricate coast-line calling for a steady hand and an undistracted mind, he nearly wore down the placid old man's patience with incessant fidgeting and captious criticisms. 'Twas a relief when with Thursday's dawn the clouds broke and the wind moderated.

Paul's spirits shot up with the mercury. The sea was heavy still—too heavy for safety, thought Porthvean—and no one else was venturing out. But Paul could sit and suck his thumbs no longer. 'Twas a fine opportunity, too, to dazzle the world with an exhibition of reckless daring and consummate seamanship. To do what no one else dared was to skim the rich cream off the milky monotony of life.

Dummy was fetched. He shook his head doubtfully, but came. Oilskins were donned, and the boat was launched in a drenching shower of spray.

Who was that on quay-head, watching their departure? Steve Polkinhorne again. And what did that malicious grin on his face mean? One didn't know, and one didn't care.

Paul steered and Dummy sculled until they were at a safe distance from shore, when the mainsail was hoisted, and off they sped, the *Swiftsure* acquitting herself gallantly, taking the big waves with grace and ease of a hunter over the fences.

They were half-way to their destination when Dummy, shifting a coil of rope, found lying underneath it a small object which had no business there. He picked it up, and after a brief examination was about to throw it overboard, when Paul, in a spirit of idle curiosity, held out his hand.

What's that?' he asked. 'Give et here for a minute.'

Dummy tossed it over, and Paul caught it.

A brief glance, and his face went grey, as the face of a man who idly picks up a curious twig, and finds that he is holding a venomous snake. His hand dropped from the tiller. The boat swerved from its course and lurched half over as a great wave struck its side. Dummy, angry and bewildered, stumbled aft and caught the tiller, pushing Paul aside. And still Paul sat and stared blankly at the insignificant bit of bone and fur in his hand.

'Mus' go back,' he muttered, when he had recovered a little. 'No use goin' on wi' this on board. We might be drowned, sure 'nough. Mus' go back.'

He laid an undecided hand on the main-sheet, withdrew it slowly, and glanced again at the thing in his hand.

'Hare's foot, sure 'nough,' he said. 'An' hare's foot, evil fortune. How did 'a come here, I wonder?'

Dummy leaned over and peered curiously at the thing, wondering what occult power it could have to strike his partner silly. It had no ominous meaning for him; the happy limits of his senses shut him off from the dark world of unspeakable shadows on the verge of which Cornish folk are treading all their lives.

'How did 'a come here?' Paul repeated. 'Somebody must ha' put en here—somebody that wished ill agin me. Who?'

The memory of Steve's malevolent visage flashed on his mind.

''Twas he!' he cried. ''Twas he, the rogue! An' he's waitin' there for us to come stavin' back, like maids from a field o' cows!'

His anger rose in a flood, battling with his superstitious misgivings. He heard Steve's triumphant chuckle, he saw his prestige wilting before the grins of all Porthvean as he slunk back, discomfited, empty-handed, without a dab or a crab to show for his vaunting prophecies. He saw that to give in was to court a repetition—endless repetitions—of this dastard blow in the dark. Unknown terrors lurked before him, defeat and derision threatened behind. White fear and red wrath grappled with each other within him ;—and the pale spectre went under.

'On we go!' he shouted in a voice to scare all apprehension away. 'No turnin' back for we! Paul Carah agin the world an' a hare's foot! I back Paul.'

The thing was still in his hand. He raised his arm to throw it far out over the water, but a thought struck him, and he slipped it into his pocket.

'There's some games two can play at, Steve, my man,' he chuckled.

The line of floats bobbed merrily ahead. 'Hurrah! Down with the sail! *We*'ll let them know!'

They brought to cleverly just over the line. With no way on, the boat began to rock and reel in the choppy sea. Paul had scarcely found his sea-legs yet, and he staggered as he stood up and made ready. His heart beat high with confidence, but the region just below seemed uneasy and timorous. Was the malevolent influence of the hare's foot making itself felt already, and was the heroic Paul going to be—perish the thought! He pulled himself together, and started hauling in, under the superintendence of Dummy.

The first dozen hooks came up as they had gone down. Then a churning, a splashing, a shout from Paul, and two small conger came up on adjacent hooks, snapping and intertwining. Then, after a long interval, a moderate-sized cod. Another cod, rather larger. An immense skate as big as a table, its great white wings flapping. They had to reeve a line over the mast before they could haul it in, and the mast bent like a whip under its weight. It covered the bottom of the boat like a carpet.

They were in for a big catch, sure enough; and hare's feet were mere foolishness, as we had thought all along.

More fish; conger, cod, ling, a fine turbot, and any amount of the small coarse fish that Porthvean lumps together under the name of 'raggle.' The boat began to sink lower in the water.

The end was almost in sight, and on the end was something heavy, something strong, something that protested vigorously against the

ignominious treatment it was suffering. Wild
with excitement, Paul signed to Dummy to lend
a hand. There was a faint stir down in the
water ; it grew nearer and increased. The two
had to redouble their efforts. Now there were
glimpses of a dark writhing column, as thick as
a stout man's leg. A flat tapering tail shot
above the surface, whirled round, and disappeared with a mighty splash. Paul hallooed,
and put all his strength into a tremendous pull ;
and out of the circle of foam which had formed
on the water, appeared a long snout like a
beast's, but fringed with minute rows of teeth
like emery paper, and two cruel, beady eyes.
Then six feet of round, sinuous, sleek, bluish-
grey body, lashing and floundering wildly.
One blow struck the boat's side, and there was
a resounding thwack like that of a flail on a
threshing-floor.

' Hooraw !' cried Paul. ' Fifty pound ef he's
an ounce !' In his excitement he did what he
should not have done, and put out his hand to
catch the creature under the throat. The tail
lashed out, Paul yelled with pain, and the hand
drooped powerless on the extended wrist.

First score to Steve.

But Dummy hauled on, and the conger,

"'Twas a duel to the death, and no one else must interfere."

lacking the leverage afforded by its native element, was in the boat in a trice, and hailing futile blows on its companions in misfortune. Dummy reached for the gaff, meaning to settle the monster by pounding it over the belly—an effective method, but only to be resorted to in the last instance, as it bruises and reddens the flesh, so lowering the market value. But Paul signed for him to desist. He was half mad with pain; he fully believed his wrist was broken; he and the conger had a private account to settle; 'twas a duel to the death, and no one else must interfere.

With his uninjured hand he pulled its head towards him by the boulter line, at the same time hooking one knee round its middle, in an attempt to grip the body between his legs. As he did so the boat gave a lurch. He stumbled, and in trying to regain his footing, trod on the slippery mass of fish beneath him. Down he went, and which was Paul and which was conger was difficult to tell. Two or three unsuccessful attempts, and he was up again, his eyes flaming, his chest heaving, his flesh tingling with the conger's vindictive blows. Seizing the line again, he nipped the creature's body in the crook of the half-disabled arm.

I

Holding it firmly against his side, regardless
of blows showered on his legs, he was able to let
the line go and clutch the conger round the throat.
Then, with a vigorous effort he got up against a
thwart, and, watching his opportunity, pinned
the lower part of the slimy, writhing body
between his two knees and the edge of the
thwart. Now he had a triple grip of the creature : by his hand at its throat, and by his
arm and knees on its body in two places. 'Twas
a dead-lock ; he could do no more.

'Knife, quick, and slit his chuck!' he gasped
to Dummy, forgetting that he could not hear.
But Dummy understood without words. With
his knife out he advanced and slit the conger's
throat from side to side. Then he tugged at
the line ; the lower jaw was torn across, and
the hook came out at the cut. Paul let go, and
the fish fell with a wet slap on the others. Life
was · in it yet, but its strength was ebbing.
They could let it flop and snap. The fight was
over, and Paul had won.

As soon as it was all over, the victorious
hero collapsed on a thwart and was violently
and most unheroically sick.

Second score to Steve.

Dummy grinned a little ; there is a humorous

incongruity in the spectacle of a sea-sick fisherman which it is not in human nature to resist. But he had sense and delicacy enough to compose his features when Paul sat up and 'glanced suspiciously at him. The sight of his stolid face was reassuring; but, to make matters quite safe, he was made to understand that if he waved the least hint of the humiliating occurrence to any one on shore, he would never be forgiven.

The great fish was on the last hook of all; so after overhauling the boulter, repairing and rebaiting it in the necessary places, they lowered it into the water again, hoisted sail, and started for home.

Paul took stock. On Steve's side of the account was the injured wrist and the disgraceful behaviour of his stomach. But the wrist on examination proved to have sustained no worse harm than a sprain; and the sickness was nothing, save for the shame of the thing, and that was nothing too, as nobody would know of it. On the other hand was the elating consciousness of having fought a big fight and won it, not merely against the brute strength of the great sea-beast, but against the subtler and more dreadful influence of powers invisible.

For that the thing in his pocket was solely responsible for the injuries he had suffered he never for a moment doubted. And in the boat under his feet heaved and panted four hundred-weight at least of prime fish. Two pounds were as good as transferred from Reseigh's pocket to his own. His wrist throbbed painfully, he was black and blue all over, but his heart was wild with exultation.

To crown all, a sweet stroke of revenge was in store for him. The wind had shifted when it subsided, and all the morning it had been fighting against the sea, planing the waves down. As the *Swiftsure* approached the cove, the other boats were putting out. One made straight for the returning craft, and Paul with a thrill recognised its occupants as Steve Polkinhorne and John Trembath, his partner, and just such another as he. Paul stood up, slipping off the bandage he had tied round his wrist. Steve must not know of that.

The boats passed within a biscuit throw of each other. As they crossed, Paul thrust his hand into his pocket, pulled out the hare's foot, and deftly tossed it into the other boat at Steve's feet.

' Returned wi' thanks,' he called, 'not havin'
no further use fur'n.'

There was a commotion, an outburst of loud
oath, a hurried consultation, and—yes! they
were putting about, they were ignominiously
ollowing the *Swiftsure* back into the harbour!

' Paid back in your own coin, Steve, my man !
A smart stroke, aha! 'Tis to be hoped you
hear our laughter. We make it as loud and
insulting as we can.'

CHAPTER X

HE FIGHTS A BATTLE

THERE followed a busy but comparatively uneventful time. Steve Polkinhorne, disconcerted by the failure of his first treacherous blow, made no attempt to repeat it. The weather continued fair, the trammel was put out; and with trammel and boulter, with the getting of bait, and the process of establishing himself firmly as an integral part of Porthvean society, Paul's time was fully occupied. The catches of fish averaged well for the time of year, and in the matter of sales, Reseigh was accommodating, even generous. Plainly the old chap, to whom the rest of the world cringed cap in hand, appreciated as a refreshing novelty Paul's careless independence, and realised that he was one with whom it were best to stand well.

In the Joses' cottage things went smoothly

on the whole. It is true that Paul and Jennifer were continually at loggerheads, as two such different natures must necessarily be ; but that did not prevent their friendship from progressing steadily. In their different ways they were equally free from malice. Their frequent tiffs, lacking the least taste of bitterness, were of the kind that forms the food of many healthy friendships. Of that which lies beyond friendship there was nothing. Each was frank with the other. Jennifer understood Paul, and Paul thought he understood Jennifer. Paul overlooked Jennifer's queer looks, and tolerated her queer ways with a magnanimity all his own ; and with great good humour Jennifer endured Paul's constant interference and advice on cooking, tea brewing, knitting, and other purely feminine matters. He was a man : nothing in the sphere of human affairs was foreign to him.

Dummy was a link between them. There were two suns in Dummy's sky now. Without abating an iota of his allegiance to Jennifer, he began to exhibit an almost equal devotion for this new companion, in whom even he could recognise something out of the common. Jennifer had once compared him to a dog ; and he had all the dog's intuition of character ; like the dog, he was attracted by the human picturesque. • Paul never made game of him as the others did ; more than once he had interfered to stop their idle teasing. Paul was strong and confident ; he looked one in the face. and laughed ; there were no secrets in him, even to a poor deaf and dumb fellow ; his face was an open book. And, thanks to a hint from Jennifer, he carried a store of sugar in his waistcoat pocket ; and Dummy had a pathetic weakness for sugar. Like a dog he adored Paul and followed him about. And like a master's to his faithful dog, so were Paul's feelings and behaviour towards Dummy. The adoration he took as a matter of course, well pleased with it, but not in the least touched. The poor chap was useful and amusing. By reason of his affliction he had a claim on one's compassion and forbearance. The rôle of protector was gratifying to one's pride, and exhibited one's character in a favourable light before oneself and the world. And he offered pleasant problems for the consideration of one's busy brain, not only in the continual exercise which the gesture-talk demanded, but in other matters too. He knew the tides to a minute ;

how, when a clock was an unfathomable mystery
to him? He went to chapel regularly; what
meaning could he attach to the rites of standing,
sitting, and kneeling, which were the only parts
of the service that could reach his senses? Then
was it not strange, suddenly to realise that, if
he were to gain his hearing, words and names
would have no meaning for him? He knew
Jennifer, but he didn't know she *was* Jennifer.
Paul was not Paul to him, but two windmill
arms and a head poked forward. He lived in
Porthvean, but it might be Columbus, Ioway,
for all *he* knew.

Paul often discussed these matters with
Jennifer, not only because Dummy interested
him, but because Dummy was almost the only
subject that could rouse Jennifer to anything
like loquaciousness. One may be fond of the
sound of one's own voice, without caring for
conversation to degenerate into monologue
sparsely punctuated with yes's and no's and
imperceptible gestures. It was not always
quite so bad as that with Jennifer; but still,
from the social point of view, she often left
much to be desired. But when Dummy was
the topic, she would talk, argue, interrupt, like
any other woman. 'Twas a strange trait in her

—this show of almost passionate affection for a creature that after all was only half-human. There were worthier objects about, too ; but let that pass. He was fond of Dummy himself in a rational way. And he could emphasise his fondness, both for the sake of effect, and because it propitiated Jennifer, and so promoted sociability. He liked the maid, and was willing ' to take a little trouble in order to stand well with her.

The worst of it was, one never knew in what strange light she might choose to view one's actions. Her moral code was all her own, and the perverse twists and bends in it made it impossible to forecast her behaviour in any situation whatever.

Take an instance.

An encounter with Steve Polkinhorne was inevitable sooner or later. If ever a man needed a thrashing it was he. Paul only waited for adequate provocation. It was offered, and one afternoon Paul burst in on Jennifer with a black eye and a glorious tale of war and victory.

' I've smashed the rogue! I tauld en I would, give me the chanst, an' I've done et. A fair stand-up fight, with all Porthvean lookin' on, an' I bet en—bet en up an' down. Ef I've got wan black eye he's got two. Got a bit o' raw beef handy, Jennifer? Fetch en an' clap en on while I tell 'ee all about et.'

'Steve?' asked Jennifer.

'Steve 'a es, 'course. He got the first blow in 'fore I was ready. That's how my eye's bad. But 'twas the last chanst he got. Gum! how I pounded en! He waan't stand straight for a week, I promise 'ee. Mazed weth anger I was, reg'lar fightin' mad! They were fo'ced to haul me off at last, or I might ha' killed en. Aw, 'twas grand! Pity you wadn' there to see, Jennifer; edn' nothin' like a fight to gie the women pleasure.'

Jennifer shut her eyes.

'I'm glad I wadn',' she said, shivering. 'But I'm glad you beat en, too, arter his be'aviour to Dummy.'

''A wadn' Dummy we fought over,' cried Paul. 'That's the grand part. 'Twas you!'

'Me!' she cried, stepping back.

'You. Look, I was down 'pon quay-head. Steve was up the other end o' the quay, an' John Trembath was down on the water in a boat. Steve an' John were hollerin' wan to the other, sayin' all the things they could think upon to gie me 'nnoyance. You d' knaw the way—they dedn' spake out plain, nor put a name to nothin', but they were gettin' at me all the while. Well, I dedn' pay no 'ttention, an' that made Steve mad, s'pose; for all of a sudden he put your name agin mine, an' said somethin'—I waan't tell 'ee what—'a edn' fitty for 'ee to hear. I was rampin' mad to wance. I staved up to en an', says I, "You may profane agin me so much as you plaise, soase, but the man that do spake 'bout a woman like that when I'm about has got to have a rare good hidin'. Put up your fistes, you bistly rogue," said I, dancin' round en, an' haulin' off my coat. An' wi' that, he hit me in the face, the varmen, when my arms were behind me, half out o' my sleeves, so's I couldn' guard myself. He was sorry direckly. Such a quilten' as I guv en! He waan't profane agin 'ee no more, Jennifer, you may be sure o' that!'

Now for the hero's delicious reward—the torrent of grateful words from fair lips, the homage to bravery and the commendation of virtue.

Jennifer was scarlet.

'Aw, 'tes shameful!' she exclaimed, miserably. 'Draggin' my name about the town, an' fightin' over me like two tinklers over a go-'bout woman! I shall never hauld up my head again. Paul, how could you do so?'

'Hullo!' Paul was never so astonished in his life. 'Do 'ee mean to say you're vexed, Jennifer, because I stand up for 'ee when a rogue insults 'ee?'

'Vexed!' she cried. 'I'm ready to die o' shame!'

Was this his reward?

'But, Jennifer, *I* never spoke your name! He said—'

'Do 'ee think I care what Steve Polkinhorne do say 'bout me? There edn' many good words spoken o' me over to cove. I scorn them all.'

'But, Jennifer, I couldn' sit still an' hear such words spoken of 'ee—'

'So you jumped up an' hammered them down, so's to give everybody a reason to talk about 'em. They're ready 'nough, gie them a chanst.'

Paul was too bewildered to be angry. He stood up for Dummy, and she praised him warmly. He did a like service to herself, and she showed her vexation unmistakably. Any

other maid would have been as pleased as
Punch at being the cause of a fight between
two men.   One expects inconsistency of a
woman; but this outrageous instance took
one's breath away.

Jennifer ˏwas touched by his expression of
puzzled dismay.

'There!' she said gently. 'You meant
well by en, I know; an' 'twas brave an'
generous.   I'd be thankful ef I could; an' I *am*
thankful to think you're so ready to take my
part.   But I'd rather you dedn'.   Don't 'ee
understand?   'Tes like settin' me naked 'pon
the quay, for the town to point their fingers at.
The shame do burn me like a hot iron.   Don't
'ee understand?'

Paul certainly didn't.   But he did understand
that he had received a black eye in her service,
and no thanks for reward.   And if ever he
played champion to a maid again— !

'I'm sorry you're hurted,' said Jennifer.
''Twas for me you took the blow, an' I'm sorry
an' grateful too.'

Then she might have said so at first, instead
of abusing him.   'Twas rank ingratitude, and
he wouldn't have believed it of her.   He didn't
want her thanks.   No, and he wouldn't let her

doctor his eye. It should remain as it was, a staring, many-coloured reproach to her. And for the rest of the day he maintained a sulky silence.

CHAPTER XI

HE GOES TO MARKET

THE season waned; the bad weather began
to set in. Trips to sea were fewer, and
at each trip the catches grew smaller. But
still, thanks to his busy energy, and, as he
generously admitted, to Dummy's knack of
pitching on the right spots, Paul's boat was
doing better than any of the others. And the
others didn't half like it. To tell the truth,
Paul's suddenly achieved popularity was waning.
The novelty of his presence had worn off; he
had begun to repeat his best yarns; of late he
had done nothing surprising to tickle their
palates, greedy for entertainment; in one or
two little disputes his determination not to be
imposed upon had led him into what Porthvean
considered high-handed proceedings. And now
he, a new-comer, was catching more fish than
any old hand among them, and he didn't fail to

keep the fact before their eyes, parading it indeed in a highly exasperating fashion. They began to remember that he was an interloper—a foreigner, or as good as a foreigner. Steve Polkinhorne was active ; and one active detractor can work havoc in the ranks of lukewarm friendship. Once more the old threats were heard of making the place too hot for him—not in his presence, though ; his long arms and utter fearlessness compelled unwilling respect. But certain little incidents showed which way the wind was blowing.

Whether by luck or by that queer instinct of his, Dummy had hit on a spot where fish swarmed. It was a narrow spit of sand between flat rocks, in ten fathoms of water, not half a mile from the shore—right under the noses of Porthvean, in fact. And they had never suspected its existence, which did not lessen their annoyance when Paul shot his net there day after day for a week with unvarying success. Then, as the spring tides were due, when nets, if left out, get choked with oarweed and rubbish, he brought the trammel ashore. Next morning four boats went out and shot nets in a circle round the spot, shutting him out effectually, regardless of the unwritten rule

K

which made the ground his till he shot elsewhere.

Another time the wind got up suddenly in the
night. The alarm was raised in the small
hours, and the men tumbled out and hurried
down to haul their boats up from the water to
a place of safety above the quay. The Joses'
cottage, as has been said, was at East Corner,
a kind of suburb some little way from the rest
of the village. No one had time to waste in
running across to warn Paul; that was not to
be expected. But they might have aroused
Dummy, who was close at hand; or when their
own boats were safe, they might have lent a
hand to rescue the *Swiftsure*, as common
humanity demanded. Not they: they hauled
up and went to bed; and when, half an hour
later, the roar of wind and sea woke Paul from
his sound sleep (he slept with the whole-hearted
determination of his waking moments), and he
flung on his clothes and ran across the cove,
he found the quay deserted, and the *Swiftsure*
tossing, straining, nearly full of water, waging
a solitary hopeless battle with the full force of
the Atlantic. Another ten minutes, and he
would have been too late.

'Well, Paul,' said Jim Boase next morning,

in answer to his furious reproaches, 'us dedn' like to touch her, knowin' what a p'tickler chap you are, an' how you hate to be interfered wi'.'

A dumb rage seized Paul. If he could only fix a quarrel on somebody—but no; they were eels in his grasp: no overt acts of hostility; only an ignoring, as complete as might be, of his existence. Talk was hushed, and groups melted away as he approached; nobody asked him to lend a hand at a job; if he offered to help, 'twas 'No thank 'ee, can manage very well myself.' In short, he was in Coventry, the most disagreeable spot on earth for one of his temperament.

Well, 'twas war to the knife, then. So be it; he would not shirk the battle. He had been in pretty much the same situation at his first arrival; he had fought then, and won. 'Twas bitterly disheartening, though, to have to begin all over again; and this time the opposition was keener and more organic. On the other hand, this time he was better acquainted with his ground; he knew his friends and his foes; and among the former he could count the second best man in Porthvean. Old Reseigh was as sympathetic, as touchingly affectionate in his behaviour as ever. What scandalously unjust talk there was of his hardness, his lust for money, his self-seeking craft! There never was a more amiable, disinterested old man; and Ben Jose was wilfully perverse n seeking to trace some obscure, deep-laid scheme in his charming behaviour to Paul. If he paid Paul top price for fish, if he praised and flattered him on every occasion, if he made him little presents of jam and tinned salmon, were these reasons for labelling him villain? Could no one else but Mr Jose himself recognise Paul's merits and behave accordingly?

An incident occurred about this time which heightened the disagreeable nature of the situation, besides involving a considerable disappointment.

It was Paul's habit, when things went well at sea, to reserve a fish or two for contribution to Jennifer's larder. One day, when there had been a big catch, he brought home a fine cod. It was decided that the head and shoulders should be boiled for supper, and the rest split and salted for future consumption. Jennifer at once set about scraping and cleaning it, while Paul sat and looked idly on. He saw her remove the liver, a yellowish convoluted lump, and passed a casual remark on the size of the thing.

'Gashly-lookin' truck, too, edn' 'a?' he said. 'An' no use to nobody, now Mister Cod's done wed'n.'

'Excep' for medicine,' Jennifer remarked.

'Aw ess, to be sure, we've all heerd tell o' cod-liver oil,' he said, and eyed the stuff with some curiosity.

Jennifer finished her job, and was going to throw the offal away, when Paul stopped her.

'Hauld on a bit,' he said. 'I've got a notion. Put that'—he pointed to the liver—'on a plate, an' throw the rest away.'

Jennifer did as she was bid, evincing no curiosity. If she felt any it was not her nature to express it; nor was it necessary. 'Twas superfluous trouble to question Paul when he had anything on his mind; 'twould come out soon enough without.

Returning, she found him jerking about in a high state of excitement.

'Gum, Jennifer!' he exclaimed, 'I've got a scheme. 'Tes workin' in my brain like barm in dough. Buzz, buzz et do go! Look! Take a pot, an' put in the cod's liver, an' set en over the fire.'

'How?' cried Jennifer. She had done some queer things at his behest before now, but surely this was the queerest demand of all.

'Do 'ee, there's a good maid. Gum! I'm goin' to make my fortune this time, sure 'nough. Come, bustle, an' do what I tell 'ee.'

There would be no peace till she did. With an inward protest she began to carry out his directions, while he unfolded his wonderful scheme.

'Cod-liver oil—that's my notion. Grand stuff—the doctors are hollerin' fur'n all day long. 'Tes the best kind o' trade they do knaw of, so I hear, an' there edn' nothin' but what 'a 'll cure en—wakeness o' the chest, wakeness o' the stomach, colds, sore uzzles, everythin' you can think upon. Grand stuff, I can tell 'ee; an' et do cost a brae lot o' money, so 'a b'lieve. An' here we are, throwin' et away all the year round. I'm wild to think how much I've throwed away myself—'nough to cure all Cornwall, I should think. Why, out in Canady, I heerd tell of a cod-fishery where they catched the cod just for the liver, and throwed the rest away. That'll tell 'ee! My fortune's made! When 'tes ready, I'll put en in a bottle an' take en round to the shop—no, I waan't, though, I'll

g' up to Henliston wed'n, to the chemist—he'll
knaw the vally of en better'n Reseigh—an',
"Here," I'll say, "cod-liver oil, home-made,
pure an' good!" "Name your price!" he'll
say, quicker'n you c'd say "knife."'

The stuff in the pot began to hiss and splutter,
and a most villainous odour diffused itself about
the room.

'Smells good, don't 'a?' said Paul, edging
towards the open door. 'Some strength in
that, 'a b'lieve. Stir en, Jennifer, and take the
scum off.'

Jennifer made a courageous attempt, but was
forced to retreat hurriedly.

'You're a fine wan, you are!' Paul ejaculated. ''Ere, gie me the spoon.'

A moment later he was retreating too,
spluttering and blinking.

'Et do smell a bit strong,' he admitted.
'Guess we'll liv en be for a bit.'

They stood and eyed the pot from a respectful distance, till Paul judged it had boiled
enough. Then, holding his nose, he rushed
forward, seized the pot, and carried it outside.

A glass preserve-jar was procured, and Paul
poured the precious liquid into it. Its appearance was not inviting, certainly. In colour it

was a sickly greenish yellow, with a muddy brown sediment slowly depositing at the bottom.

' Are 'ee sure 'tis cod-liver oil? ' asked Jennifer, doubtfully. ' I've seen some wance, and 'twas clear and white, like water, most, not mucky yaller stuff like this.'

' 'Tes the stren'th an' goodness of en makes et so,' Paul explained. ' Sim' me, the stuff they sell in shops edn' but poor truck : the rogues do mix en an' make en weak, because they may get a bigger profit. That's how I belong to get a good price for this. They're artful ; they d' knaw ; an' I'll let 'em see I d' knaw too. Qual'ty an' price do go together, an' this is pure an' strong. Aw, they'll jump fur'n up to Henliston ! I'll go there to-morrow, 'pon the omnibus, so I will.'

And he went. May one digress a little in order to describe the vehicle he went on? The *Paragon* was its real name, but it was better known as the *Green Snail*, by reason of its complexion and habits. In appearance it resembled as nearly as possible the Brixton omnibus of the old days before garden-seats, except that the knife-board was absent, its place being taken by two transverse benches rising one above the other behind the driver. The back part of the roof was seatless, being intended for luggage, though when the 'bus was full it generally carried a heap of sprawling, clinging humanity, too. Round the woodwork of the sides ran a string of names of places, painted in yellow against the dingy green. The list included every town of importance within twenty miles of Henliston. Not that the 'bus ever ran to these places; in all the long years of its existence it had never adventured its wheels off the Henliston road, and in all probability it would never do so till the hour when it fell to pieces. But the Celtic imagination—or call it foresight—of the builder had made allowances for every possibility, even the remotest. Somebody *might* charter the vehicle for a circular tour through West Cornwall; besides, the formidable array of far-off names added dignity and inspired respect. They were a certificate of merit, so to speak, proclaiming to the world what the *Paragon* was capable of if it tried.

The owner and driver, Herklous Rutter by name, was a man of autocratic temper and inflexible punctuality. The 'bus was advertised to run to Henliston twice a week, on Wednesdays and Saturdays, starting at two precisely. At one o'clock the horses were harnessed, and the *Paragon* driven to the starting-place. At a quarter past one Herklous Rutter descended into the streets of Porthvean and rapped at the door of every house in turn, imploring the inmates to hurry up if they were coming. Also, that no one who happened to be out of doors should have an excuse for tardy arrival, he carried a whistle, which he blew at frequent intervals. Having thus sifted Porthvean from end to end, he returned, driving his passengers captive before him. When they were all seated he mounted the box. It would then be ten minutes to two, perhaps a little earlier, perhaps a little later. Now there was nothing to wait for; a less punctual man would have started at once. Not so Herklous; he had a reputation to maintain. At two, and not till two, he jammed his hat firmly over his eyes, cracked his whip and jerked the reins. The *Paragon* gave a mighty lurch, as if it was being torn out of the road by invisible roots, the passengers breathed a silent prayer that the old concern might last out one journey more, and off they started. If a belated voyager should turn up then, he could not hope for Herklous to pull up and wait for him; he must mend his pace and catch Herklous up as best he could ; and it took a pretty brisk walker to do *that*, let me tell you.

The journey of eleven miles took two hours and a half, no more, no less. At every cross-road, and at every wayside house or cluster of houses, Herklous drew up and waited from one minute to ten, according to programme. At Ponsanveneth, half-way, there was a somewhat longer break in the journey, while Herklous got down and went across two fields to pay a call on his sister, who had married a downser. If, in spite of careful calculations, there was any fear of arriving before the advertised time, Herklous adjusted matters by walking his horses along levels, as well as up and down the hills.

The *Paragon's* holding capacity was little short of miraculous. Starting from Porthvean apparently as full of fisher-folk as it could hold, at every stoppage it absorbed a fat farm-wife with her baskets ; or an equally bulky farmer, his pockets bulging with sample-bags, or a maid and her sweetheart, bent on mild dissipation and a taste of town life. But a pair of the latter only counted as one, or what were a chap's knees made for ? Herklous calculated

in reaching Henliston with double the number
he started with, and he was seldom out.
Packed inside like pilchards in a barrel,
swarming outside like flies on a preserve pan,
they jolted and joked, lurched and laughed, as
good-humoured, merry a company as you
would find anywhere.

'Twas a happy journey for Paul. He sat
on the box beside Herklous, and whatever
Herklous's attitude towards him as a private
individual might be, in his official seat he was
strictly neutral, recognising no differences,
sinking all prejudice, affably conversible with
all alike. In the highest spirits—as who would
not be who carried a prospective fortune in his
pocket?—Paul chatted away, yarning about
coach-rides in the Rockies, advising Herklous
on the management of his team, and unable, in
spite of himself, to refrain from frequent
mysterious references to the object of his
journey, and to the wonderful, not-to-be-
divulged contents of the parcel he carried.
Ostensibly addressing Herklous, he took care
to keep his voice well above conversational
pitch, blissfully conscious of open-mouthed
silence among the country folk behind him. At
the journey's end, as he swung off the coach,

he thrilled to feel the eyes of all the passengers fixed curiously on him, following him up the street; and a sneering remark of 'What may-game's the chap up to now?' uttered by a Porthvean man, only put the crown on his bounding elation.

He was to have returned as he went; but the *Paragon* did not arrive in Porthvean till ten o'clock, and it was not later than half-past seven when he flung into the Joses' kitchen and dropped on a chair. Mr Jose looked up inquiringly from his map and Jennifer from her knitting.

'Back already?' said the old man. 'What luck?'

'Haul' tongue!' exclaimed Paul irritably.

For a minute or two he sat scowling in silence; then it all came out with a rush.

These chemists! They were all rogues or fools, if they weren't both. Sold it? No, he hadn't; the ignorant rascals wouldn't look at it. One had burst out laughing in his face; another had threatened to kick him out of the shop, if he didn't take himself off with his filthy stuff. *They* didn't want to cure people; cured people wouldn't need their services; 'twas their interest to sell poison; they were a gang of murderers, slowly sapping the life out of the country with their virulent drugs; they ought to be in prison, the lot of them. Rogues all! A benefactor to his race offered them the elixir of life, and they rejected it with outward contempt, with inward panic at the vision evoked of shutters put up in the face of a restored, rejuvenated world. Where was the bottle? He had thrown it into the gutter in a fit of disgust. Why had he walked home? Because he didn't want to be plagued with a coach-load of inquisitive fools. Fools and rogues; where was the honest man among them?

Mr Jose strove to soothe him with expressions of indignant sympathy; Jennifer, subtler in her methods, set supper before him without delay. The pork and potatoes calmed him somewhat; the bread and jam restored his good humour; and when the corn-cob was lit, he was himself again, and ready with a new scheme.

Wish I hadn' throwed et away,' he said. 'Twould ha' done fine to oil my say-boots wi'. Gum! I'll catch another cod to-morrow. 'A 'll keep my feet dry, ef 'a don't make my fortune.'

But he was not to dismiss the matter so lightly. Emanating, as it is supposed, from the bar of the 'White Horse,' where the Henliston tradesmen meet nightly for recreative chat, a farcical tale arose and spread over town and country. It reached Porthvean, and Porthvean found itself possessed of a most potent weapon of offence against Paul. Scowls he could endure ; blows he could repay with interest ; against ridicule he was powerless, a squirming, impotent worm.

Affectionate inquiries about the market price of cod set him foaming at the mouth. Mock discussions on pharmaceutry, with special reference to cod-liver oil, drove him to shun the neighbourhood of his fellow-men. They were quick to discover the effectiveness of their new weapon, and you may be sure they did not allow it to rust for want of use. Great things were expected of Jim Boase, and he upheld his reputation. He went about racked with the hollow cough of the consumptive, calling aloud for medicine to ease his pain. And there was only one remedy that could give relief, and 'twas a remedy the name of which Paul wished he had never heard.

CHAPTER XII

HE KISSES A MAID

MR JOSE watched the growth of friendly relations between Paul and Jennifer with chuckling delight. The great desire of his later years seemed in a fair way to be realised. When man and maid plant the tree of brotherhood together, and water it continually with confidential talk, it will not be long before buds of love appear, to become in time blossoms fit for the decoration of the matrimonial altar. It was not in him to resist the temptation to make little forcing experiments, which in his clumsy fingers were apt to produce anything but the desired effect.

It was his invariable custom every Sunday after dinner to take the big family Bible from the side table where it reposed during the week, and retire with it into the grim little parlour, where he would sit bolt upright on one of the rigid chairs, facing his wife's portrait, the Bible on his knees, reading, meditating, dozing now and again, and communing with the spirit of the departed. For it was his belief that she was permitted to pay a weekly visit to her earthly home every holy day from two till four. (Pardon the grotesque touch; there was nothing grotesque or irreverent in it to the simple old man.) Hence his scrupulous care to keep everything in the room exactly as it had been in the days of her lifetime. The notion of a spirit purged of all earthly passions was inconceivable to him. Something of the late Mrs Jose's devotion to her best room must still cling to her; something, too, of the temper that had brooked no interference with its inflexible arrangement. Her anger of old had been a thing to flee from; how much more so her ghostly wrath!

All through the afternoon he sat there, shut off from the world, as in an ante-chamber to the palace of the Hereafter. Sometimes he would come out, his homely face shining, with stories of a voice heard, of a soft hand laid on his shoulder, of glimpses caught of a bright thing floating. Paul and Jennifer remained in

the kitchen, talking in whispers, vaguely conscious of a supernatural presence.

One Sunday afternoon, the old man, with
the Bible tucked under his arm, and his hand on
the parlour door, about to push it open, paused
and looked back on the two young people.
They made a delightfully domestic picture, sure
enough—Jennifer looking out of the window, with
her elbows on the table and one hand support-
ing her cheek ; Paul by the fire, smoking, his
long legs sprawling over half the room. Things
were going swimmingly, to be sure ; but a
diplomatic fillip would not be amiss.

'Mus' liv 'ee alone now for a bit,' he said.
'But don't s'pose you've any objection to *that*,
from what I mind o' *my* young days. Don't
be bashful, Paul ; an,' Jennifer, don't 'ee be
teasy.'

With a knowing wink he disappeared.

Jennifer, looking up with a gesture of annoyance, caught a broad grin on Paul's face. She
started to her feet.

'I'm goin' out for a walk,' she said abruptly.

'Are 'ee, though ?' said Paul. 'Well, I
don't much fancy stoppin' in here alone '—here
he glanced at the parlour door—'so I'll come
wi' 'ee.'

'No, you waan't,' said Jennifer decidedly.
'I'm goin' alone.'

'How?' asked Paul. 'You're brave an'
soshabble to-day, edn' you?'

'I don't wish no Sunday strolls wi' young
men,' said she. 'Folks 'll talk nonsense.'

'Pouf! Let 'em talk,' said he. (''Twill
be fun if they do,' he thought.)

'I hate to be talked about,' said she.

'Do 'ee, now?' he said, with unfeigned
surprise. She hated it! And to his taste it
gave life half its savour, and that the sweeter
half.

'Ess. 'Specially in *that* way,' said she,
growing red.

'What way?' grinned he.

Her Sunday hat was on the table, where she
had laid it on her return from morning chapel.
She caught it up, and was retreating upstairs.
Paul intercepted her, and seized the hat by the
brim, laughing. A walk with Jennifer was no
great allurement, but he was not to be thwarted
and contemptuously thrust aside by any maid
in creation.

'Let go,' said Jennifer, under her breath.

'Not without you promise to let me come.'

'No!' she declared, tugging at the hat.

'I will, then, whether you've a mind to or no,' he insisted, piqued at her obstinacy.

'Never while I do live!' she averred, trying to wrench the hat out of his hand.

'No, you don't!' cried Paul, laughing boisterously and tugging back. 'Pulley-haul!'

There was a tearing sound, and half the brim came away in Paul's hand. Abashed and disconcerted, he strove to smother his confusion with a louder laugh.

'Gum! what a joke!' he exclaimed.

Never was a woman so free from dressy vanity as Jennifer; but the wanton destruction of her best hat and Paul's brutal laughter were too much for her composure. She sank on a chair and began to cry.

''Ere, what's this? Hauld on a bit, Jennifer!' exclaimed Paul, evincing all a man's irritated discomposure at the sight of feminine tears.

'You're a brute,' sobbed Jennifer, 'an' I'll never spake ti' 'ee again—never!'

Paul began to pace up and down, his emotions shifting, and each change producing a muttered sentence.

'So much your fault as mine. How dedn'

'ee let go?' He could think of no other word of justification. 'Twas a weak one, too.

'What a fuss over a shabby auld hat!' Women are petty creatures. It takes a man to rise superior to trivial misfortunes.

'Jennifer, I give 'ee my word I dedn' mane to do et!' 'Twas handsomely said; but the perverse creature wept on silently, and took no notice whatever.

'Jennifer, I'll buy 'ee a new wan, twice as good, nex' week, so I will.' There! what more did she want? A good deal, seemingly; for she gave no sign. The sound of a long-drawn sob made something within him prick and tingle unpleasantly. *Was* he a brute? He had been a bit too rough, certainly.

'Jennifer, don't be vexed. I'm sorry, that I am.' An apology? Paul Carah owning himself in the wrong? And it didn't hurt him either; on the contrary, he felt a delightful glow—virtuous magnanimity, no doubt.

Still no sign.

'Jennifer, forgi'e me, will 'ee, an' be friends?'

Still mute? Well, he wasn't going to beg again; and he didn't care a rap. And he didn't feel as miserable as a tinkler's cur; on the contrary, he was in the highest of spirits—witness his merry whistling.

The sound of a scraping chair came from the adjoining room. Jennifer sat up, and hurriedly wiped her eyes.

'Stop whistlin',' she said. 'You're vexin' da. He'll be out direckly.'

'Let en,' said Paul, between two staves.

'Stop, I tell 'ee,' urged Jennifer. 'You don't knaw how p'tickler da is 'bout Sunday be'aviour, f'rall his quiet ways. He'll turn 'ee out, as like as not. Not that I care ef 'a do, so don't think et. But da mustn' be vexed. I beg of 'ee, stop.'

'Say you do forgi'e me, then, or I whistle in the face of en,' said the cunning Paul.

The latch of the door gave a preliminary rattle.

'Quick!' whispered Paul, bending over her. 'Quick, an' the canary gets the fault.'

'Ess, then, I forgive 'ee,' she murmured, yielding to circumstance.

An absurd, irrational impulse, in which deliberate intention had no part, he would swear, made Paul stoop still lower and kiss the hair over her forehead. She flushed an angry crimson, just as the parlour door flew open and disclosed Mr Jose.

'What ded I hear?' he said sternly. 'Profane whistlin' on a Sunday?'

'Whistlin'?' said the unblushing Paul. 'Law no! Must ha' been the canary you heerd. The li'll chap's been hollerin' fit to put one deef.'

''Twas a tune I heerd,' said Mr Jose severely, 'a profane weeky-day tune. An' you tell me 'twas the canary?'

'Aw ess, 'twas he, right 'nough,' Paul assured him. 'Smart li'll chap. This long while I've noticed en when I've been whistlin', listenin' with his heed cocked on wan side, takin' et all in. Sim' me he'd a mind to surprise us all with his cleverness.'

Mr Jose looked doubtfully at Paul. Then he stepped from the doorway and peered up at the cage.

'Never heerd tell o' no s'ch thing,' he muttered, shaking his head in a puzzled way. 'Strange, to be sure. Wouldn' ha' b'lieved et.'

Only half convinced, he was returning, when he caught sight of Jennifer's flushed, tear-stained face. She seemed greatly agitated;

now he looked, so did Paul. And when the door opened, had they not been very close together, he bending over her? There was only one inference possible. The old man's face cleared; the reprehensible behaviour of the canary went out of his mind, and he smiled a cunning smile.

'There! I dedn' mane to interrupt 'ee,' he said. 'Don't mind me; get along with your chat. I'm goin' back.'

He trotted off into the parlour, rubbing his hands gleefully, and carefully shutting the door behind him.

'Grand!' he said to himself. 'I knawed they only wanted a little pushin' an' managin'. Grand, so 'a es!'

In the kitchen an embarrassed silence reigned. The thoughts of both dwelt on one thing—the kiss. Paul was wondering what on earth had possessed him to act so foolishly and imprudently. 'Twas a generous impulse, no doubt, springing from the sight of her distress, and calculated to allay it more quickly and completely than anything else. But how rash! He knew these women, 'twas a short cut in their minds from a kiss to a ring. *Absit omen!* She was a sensible maid; surely she would never take it seriously. 'Twas her way, though, to take things seriously. If she did—! He liked her well enough at times; as a friend she was tolerable, even desirable; but as a sweetheart! No, when we want one, 'tis to be hoped we can find a better looking one, and a better tempered one, one that will look up to us more, laugh more readily at our jokes, appreciate better our unique merits, and not keep such a sharp eye for the few infinitesimal faults in our character.

Jennifer was angry with herself because she was not angrier with Paul. Something unknown and terrible had come over her; she knew not what. He had torn her hat, he had mocked and insulted her, he had lied outrageously to her father, and she had weakly submitted and acquiesced. She hated herself for it. And this masterful, overbearing fellow, who strove to bend her to his will by sheer brute force, did she not hate him too? And if not, why not? Her tears had left her weak and passive, and over her forehead was a spot that burned. Confused emotions whirled within her, one she could recognise—'twas shame, overwhelming shame; the others she could fit no names to.

He was strangely silent. She peeped furtively up at him. He stood biting his lip, and
staring moodily into the fire. He had her at
his mercy, and he didn't know, or didn't
care. She hated the brutal fellow. And he
was kind and tender with her Dummy, too.
Father was fond of him. He stamped and
shouted and boasted ; he was as conceited as a
cloamen cat ; she detested him. Yet he was
strong and brave ; he had done things to excuse,
if not to justify, his conceit and boasting.
When Steve insulted her he had not stopped to
weigh the consequences, but had flown to fight
in defence of her good name. Small thanks he
had got from her for that. He could own he
was in the wrong too ; just now he had humbly
apologised. And he had gained her pardon.
But how? By a mean trick. And then he
had kissed her ; not on the face, though—thank
goodness for that. But he had kissed her.
No doubt he had kissed maids before ; he had
dropped hints to that effect in a casual, joking
way, as if 'twere nothing. No one had ever
kissed her before. Did he realise how it
shocked and pained her ? She wished to do
him justice. Could she blame him for doing
what another girl would consider in the light

of a joke, and dismiss from her mind with a laugh and a blush? Ah! but to be kissed by a talkative boaster. All the world would know of it. Yes, she hated him.

Unasked, unlooked-for, he had come splashing into the quiet current of her life, where no other man had entered, save her father. After her first mistrustful alarm she had acquiesced, and from indifference had passed to calm, openeyed, tolerant liking. And now at a touch he had sprang to gigantic proportions, filling her horizon, blotting out all else. There was something in her that magnified him portentously, merits, faults and all. The image, with its terrible promise of persistence, possessed and overwhelmed her.

She ventured to peep at him again. He did not seem elated. That frown might mean bewilderment, or depression, or shame, but not the pluming coxcomb's vanity she feared.

He was peeping round too, and their eyes met.

'Jennifer,' he said hesitatingly, 'we — we waan't say no more 'bout this; we'll forget everythin' that happened, eh?'

She was surprised and grateful.

'Ess, Paul,' she said in a low voice. 'Best to do so.'

'I dedn' mane to—to do that,' he stammered ; 'an' I caan't think what made me. 'A wadn' in my mind to do so, an' I dedn' mane nothin' by en—nothin' at all.'

She believed him, and she was glad—yes, she was sure she was glad to hear it.

'"Friends an' no nonsense?"' quoted Paul, with a half laugh.

'"Friends an' no nonsense,"' replied Jennifer solemnly.

CHAPTER XIII

HE REPROVES A MAID

ABOUT the second week in November north-easterly gales set in. After waiting a few days Porthvean drew up its boats and resigned itself to a long rest of four months, thankful that the elements had delayed so long before announcing winter. It came as a relief to Paul; already he was beginning to weary of this eternal shooting and. pulling up of nets and lines; he pined for a temporary change of occupation, above all for one that would not necessitate constant appearances in the village, where the finger of ridicule was as the finger on a sign-post, permanent, fixed, ever pointing Paulward.

There was plenty to do. A fisherman's rest in winter is only a rest from the fight with the waves; it must not be supposed that he remains idle meanwhile. With the spring comes crabbing time, and the pots must be ready. A set or 'fleet' of pots numbers seventy-two, all to be renewed yearly; and two pots a day make hard work. And before they are made the materials must be procured. At Porthvean this meant ten-mile tramps over the moors to the nearest osier-bed, days of hard labour up to one's knees in a swamp, cutting and trimming the withies, and weary journeys back through the winter darkness with a heavy faggot on one's back.

Then there were other long tramps over crofts and copses, selecting and cutting sticks of hazel, blackthorn, and furze, afterwards to be trimmed down into 'preens,' the forked skewers used for fixing the bait in the pots. When the fleet was finished there was the great store-pot to be made, three days' labour in itself: and after that the other gear must be seen to, nets rebarked and mended, new hooks fitted to lines, and new lines to hooks, the boat tarred and painted, and fifty other jobs, big and small, attended to. Paul's hands, and Dummy's too, would be full till long after Christmas.

How did matters stand now? Neither well nor ill. Six weeks of fishing had resulted in a gain of twelve pounds. A third share, four

pounds, went to Dummy. Incidental expenses
had absorbed two more. The six remaining,
added to five he had in hand, made eleven. But
there would be none coming in for four
months; and there was a lot to pay out—so
much to the owner of the withy-bed, so much
to Reseigh for the ropes—three hundredweight
—on which to string the pots. Bark, tar, more
hooks, personal expenses—he would be lucky
if by next March he had two sovereigns to
jingle together. Well, better that than nothing; better nothing than the millstone of debt
under which the rest of Porthvean groaned.
They might harass him, and mock him, but he
could laugh back; he was a free man, and
Reseigh's frown had no terrors for him.

What was up with Jennifer he couldn't
think. Like the magnanimous fellow he was,
he had quite forgotten the little incident of the
Sunday hat. While the memory was fresh he
had felt some constraint and uneasiness in her
presence, but it had soon faded. With schemes
and ideas pushing, shouldering, playing leap-
frog in one's brain all day long, the trivial
traces of a tiff and a kiss are soon obliterated.
He was quite ready, even generously anxious,
to re-establish their relations on the old friendly

basis. But Jennifer had changed—unaccount-
ably changed. From the calm, serious, steadfast girl he had known before, and grown to
like, even to respect in a way, she had suddenly developed into a creature of moods. One
day she would be her old self; the next, she
was pettish and irritable, taking offence at
little things, snapping out sarcasms. Then
again a fit of obstinate silence would come over
her; if Paul spoke, she would make no answer;
or she would avoid him altogether, retreating
to her room when they were left alone together. The crab-pots were a-making; Dummy
came round daily to work in the out-house
which Paul had appropriated for his store-room
and workshop. And on Dummy she lavished
an effusive, desperate tenderness, alien, one
would have thought, to her nature. Dummy
trod a maze of chuckling bliss; Paul betrayed
some irritation at the foolishness of it all; and
the more he fretted, the more she persisted.
Sometimes he felt her eyes on him; he looked
round and met them; they were the eyes of
the hare in the springe. One would say that
some violent struggle was going on within her.
Still waters run deep; bubbles rising to the
surface give indication of a disturbance; but

to the nature of that disturbance they yield no clue—at least they yielded none to Paul, puzzle as he might.

If Paul was puzzled, Mr Jose was deeply distressed. A fixed idea may blind one up to a point, but there may come a time when stubborn facts block the way, and one is forced to open one's eyes. Convinced of the substantial nature of his hopes, sure of their near fulfilment, at first he regarded Jennifer's unexampled behaviour as a favourable symptom, quoting to himself fragments of secular lore touching the capriciousness of maids under the influence of the tender passion. But as time went on, he began to fidget, discerning no signs of progress ; rather did they seem to be drifting apart. In his anxiety he sank so low as to spy on them, departing noisily from the house and creeping back on tip-toe to listen at the door ; for they might be playing a double game, as lovers will, teasing him by feigning indifference in his presence. But either they were moodily silent, or the few words he overheard could not be twisted by the liveliest imagination into expressions of tenderness. He tried his famous diplomacy once more, with the lamentable result of driving Jennifer upstairs

M

with a slammed door behind her. Jennifer slamming doors! 'Twas a portent. The fabric of his dream-castle shivered and melted at the sound.

For a while he kept suspicious watch on Paul. If the fellow was behaving badly to his dear little maid—trifling with her—! But Paul's behaviour was unexceptionable. He seemed as puzzled by her demeanour, as ignorant of its motive, as Mr Jose himself. If he betrayed no ardent despair, he tried several times very handsomely to placate her when she was more pettish than usual. No; the fault, if any, must be Jennifer's. He attempted a grave, gentle remonstrance, and almost lost his temper at the show of obstinate, sullen silence with which she met it. He began to think it was a case for the doctor.

Then Paul, ignorant of the old man's attempt, tried his hand also. One morning he and Dummy were at work in the out-house. There was a tidy pile of pots in the corner now, and three or four were being added to it daily. They sat face to face, each with the pot in progress fixed between his knees. 'Twas a bright winter morning; the sunlight streamed in at the door, and with it came the limpid crystal song of a red-breast, and now and again the glad yelp of a gull or the barking clamour of a company of jackdaws, giving tongue as they swept by. The shed was full of the sweet sappy odour of the freshly peeled withies. Paul whistled as he worked, now and then waving an encouraging hand to Dummy, or getting up to examine his work and compare its progress with that of his own. Not that Dummy required supervision ; he was the best weaver of pots in Porthvean, and he knew it, and took a simple pride in his work. He was slow, as at most things ; Paul could finish three pots to his two ; but Paul's was prentice work in comparison, impatient and inartistic, all ragged ends and irregular curves. Dummy's pots were miracles of craftmanship, strong, neat, mathematically exact of dimension, every constituent rod and twig selected with judgment and interwoven in the fabric with meticulous nicety. 'Twas a sight to see him bending over his work, his lips pursed up, the wrinkles coming and going on his face, his bald head shining as if his brain was perspiring, his stumpy hairy hands moving steadily in and out, in and out among the withies.

Jennifer came out of the kitchen, hovered

about the out-house door, and finally entered.
Totally ignoring Paul's greeting, she sat down
on a trestle with her back to him and her face
to Dummy. Paul saw Dummy look up and
grin delightedly, his hands keeping busy at the
pot. Then Jennifer made some gestures.
Dummy's grin expanded; his hands flashed
up, went to Jennifer's shoulder, to his own
breast, out seaward, and up into the air with
two fingers erect from each clenched fist.
Four-master again, thought Paul.

Dummy returned to his work; but he had
hardly done so before Jennifer's hands were
waving again. Answering at first only with
smiles and nods, Dummy was presently se-
duced into pushing the pot away from between
his feet, and entering into an animated conversation.

After a few minutes Paul felt called upon to
enter a protest.

'Jennifer,' he said, 'you're hinderin'
Dummy. He'll never finish that pot this
mornin' ef you don't liv en be. He edn' like
we; he caan't talk an' work too.'

She looked slowly round, stared him in the
face for a moment, and turned back without a
word. Her behaviour had been particularly

trying for some days past, and this was the climax. Paul got up and stood by the door, guarding it. There should be no evasion; he was going to have it out with her there and then.

'Look, Jennifer,' he said, firmly but kindly, for he liked the maid. She was plain, she was teasy, she showed him scanty respect, but after all he liked her. 'Look, Jennifer. I don't knaw what's come ti' 'ee this good while. You edn' be'avin' at all proper, an' I look to knaw the manen of et.'

No answer; no sign that she heard him. To and fro went her hands, and she laughed with a feverish gaiety in answer to Dummy's perpetual chuckle.

Paul persevered. The attitude of grave, temperate reproof sat well on him, he thought; 'twas the experienced man of the world admonishing the petulant, ignorant child.

'You're vexin' your da, an' you're vexin' *me*. You never used to be so. As well-be'aved a maid as ever I met, you were. How are you so teasy, slightin' those that wish 'ee well, an' look to be trated well by 'ee?'

'Twas well put, plain, not too forcible, and nicely rounded. But she might have been a

stone for all the effect it had on her. Paul bit
his lip. He could be angry, but he wouldn't.
There was a problem set—to make her speak ;
he was going to solve it. She was a maid ;
he would abandon remonstrance for tender
appeal.

'Come, Jennifer,' he said softly ; 'you're
vexed about somethin'—vexed an' wretched.
We're friends, edn' we ? Dedn' we agree to
that ? Won't you tell your friend what 'a
es ?'

Still no answer ; but her hands dropped on
her lap. He edged round behind Dummy till
he had a view of her face. Her eyes were cast
down, and her mouth worked. Poor little
maid ! He felt sorry for her, but she must
be made to feel the error of her ways.

''A edn' fitty 'tall to scorn your friends, an'
slight them so,' he said.

Her eyes went up ; they were wild and hard.

''Edn' *you* I do scorn !' she cried harshly.

'Who, then ?'

No reply.

'Who, then ?' he repeated. Her evident
distress moved him more than he could have
thought possible. He forgot his crafty tactics ;
it was with a genuine impulse of tenderness

that he moved towards her and laid his hand gently on her shoulder.

'Jennifer, dear,' he said appealingly, 'won't you tell me your trouble?'

'Never!' she cried; and for the second time in his experience of her she burst into tears.

Paul was quite upset, and completely at sea. Not long ago he would have applied the gauge of his vanity, and attributed her behaviour to a flattering, if commonplace motive. But now the thought never entered his head. He knew Jennifer; she was not as other maids were. She could be a friend to a man; he was convinced she could be nothing more. But whatever the cause of her emotion might be, it really hurt him and touched him deeply.

'Don't 'ee cry,' he murmured incoherently, kneeling beside her and stroking her hair. 'Don't 'ee cry, my dear; it vexes me so, you caan't think. Don't vex your friend, Jennifer. Come, tell me all about et, an' ef I can help 'ee—'

She shook her head and sobbed on. Paul looked despairingly about him.

There came a diversion from an unexpected quarter. Paul heard an angry growl at his elbow. He turned, and there was Dummy, whose existence he had forgotten. And what on earth was up with Dummy?

Dummy, rapt from the seventh heaven by Paul's interruption, had returned to his work for a moment, only to relinquish it immediately. Paul's protesting attitude and Jennifer's obstinate silence puzzled him. Were his two adored ones quarrelling? He watched them narrowly. He saw a question, a vehement reply, and then Paul's hand on Jennifer, and Jennifer in tears. His dear mistress weeping? He was frantic at the sight. What was distressing her? Slowly he worked it out. It must be something Paul had done or said. His anger blazed. He loved and admired Paul, but Jennifer was first by a long way in his affections. He jumped up, growling; and Paul looked round to encounter two glaring wrathful eyes. Instinctively he retreated a step. Dummy rushed to Jennifer, and stooped over her, fondling her and making soft cooing noises. He rushed back to Paul and shook his fist in his face, jabbering fiercely. Jennifer claimed him again. Her face was hidden; he lifted it gently and pored on it. What he read there jumped him to his feet, his rage redoubled. He advanced on Paul with unmistakably hostile intentions.

'Stand back!' cried Paul, and tried to explain. 'Twas explaining to a wild bull. On came Dummy, mad with fury; and Paul retreated before him—not from fear; strength for strength he was more than a match for Dummy, without taking science into account; but he didn't wish to harm the faithful, blundering creature. So he retreated as Dummy advanced. Round the shed they circled. Paul realised the ridiculousness of his position; he couldn't actually run away; he was reluctant to stand and come to blows. There was only one course open to him, humiliating, but the only one—an appeal to Jennifer.

'Jennifer,' he exclaimed, 'call him off, or I'm forced to knock him down!'

Jennifer looked up, saw Paul's look of helpless disgust at the fantastic war-dance he was taking compulsory part in, and burst into a fit of hysterical laughter. Dummy stopped dead; his anger cleared away, he darted back to her side and began to express his delight at the change in her mood by a whirl of extravagant gestures.

Paul was alarmed by the laughter more than

he had been by the tears. He started forward,
thought better of it, opened his mouth to speak,
thought better of that too, and finally turned
and went slowly into the garden. Best leave
her alone for a bit, he thought.

He leaned by the house door considerably
shaken by the scene he had just gone through.
Poor little maid! what could have upset her
so? Some genuine trouble it must be; no
slight matter could thus disturb the deep calm
of her nature. She wouldn't tell; she seemed
ashamed to tell. 'Edn' *you* I do scorn.'
Herself then? Why? He recalled what he
could remember of the whole affair, and of the
events preceding it. No; he could see no
light. Poor little maid! He was glad that
something had impelled him to treat her
tenderly. He could do it with safety; there
was no nonsense about her, and she would not
misunderstand.

Why, here she came, quite collected, but
with downcast eyes. She approached him.

'Feel better now?' he said encouragingly.
' That's right.'

'Paul,' she said in a low voice, 'I wish to
ask your pardon for my be'aviour since—for
my be'aviour lately. You're right, I haven'

treated 'ee fitty. Ef you do forgi'e me, I'll be thankful, an' I'll try to be'ave different.'

'There, that's all right,' he cried heartily, 'an' we'll say no more. But ef you'd only tell me—'

'Don't!' she interrupted. 'Don't ask me, for I can never tell 'ee. 'Twas only a maid's foolishness; we're weak creatures, you d' knaw.'

'So you are,' admitted Paul. 'But I didn' think et o' *you*, Jennifer, an' I caan't make it out. Why, 'twas as ef we were swettards, an' I'd slighted 'ee!'

She cast a swift affrighted glance on him. He was laughing at the absurd notion. She dropped her eyes, and laughed too—a queer little laugh.

'I—I edn' that sort, you d' knaw,' she said.

'That's what I say,' said Paul, still laughing. 'An' I'll tell 'ee what, Jennifer. 'Tes a good thing to meet with a maid like you, wance in a way, that thinks as you do 'bout all that.' He waved his hand comprehensively. 'I dedn' think so at first; I saw you wadn' like other maids, an' that puzzled me. An' when I'm puzzled I'm vexed—that's me. But now I'm

glad you're so. Look! I've gone swettardin'
before now; 'twas fun for a while, but, my
ivers! how sick I got o' the fullishness of en,
'fore 'twas done! But you! why, you're as
good as a man 'most. Tell 'ee, I do think a
brae lot of 'ee. Friendship, aha! better'n all
the swettardin' in the world, edn' 'a?'

'Ess, to be sure,' she said in a clear voice,
and looked him in the face and smiled. She
was very pale, and as she smiled she laid her
hand on the door.

'Paul,' she said faintly, 'I don't feel very
well. Sim' me, I'm a bit upset. I'll go over
stairs an' lie down for a bit.'

'Do 'ee, now,' Paul urged. 'Don't trouble
'bout denner just yet,' he called after her. 'I
shaan't mind ef 'tes a bit late this wance.'

You see he could be generous, and self-
sacrifice was not altogether unknown to him.

CHAPTER XIV

HE GOES DIGGING

JENNIFER kept her word, and dropped her incomprehensible behaviour for good. She was not quite the same as before, though; quieter than ever, more subdued, wonderfully gentle with everybody, especially with Paul. The pride seemed to have gone out of her.

Christmas came and went in peace. The pots were finished, the gear all mended and stored away in the out-house, and by the beginning of February little remained to be done on the seaward side of affairs. Landward, so far as human intercourse went, things were quiet, almost stagnant. At home there was no excitement to be got out of Jennifer. Mr Jose was sanguine again since the fresh change in domestic relations, but had grown to doubt the wisdom of interference in affairs of the heart, which are proverbially ticklish subjects for a third person to meddle with. So he lay low and let things take their course. With the cove one had little traffic. One stepped across now and again to buy matches or what not, and to chat with the amiable Reseigh, the one just man in a den of rogues. The others were in Coventry.

Paul's restless spirit sought about for something to do, for some one or something to battle with, manœuvre against, cajole, astonish, and what not. And some one he found right under his nose, no less a one than Mother Earth herself. Her winter sleep is brief in Cornwall—a mere doze, which a single sunny day is enough to disturb, even in January. By the first days of February she is wide awake.

Early one morning Paul came out and leaned over the garden gate, waiting for breakfast. It was a bright day, soft and fresh after a night of rain. From the ground arose that sweetest, most intoxicating of odours, the odour of moist earth in spring sunshine; and everywhere on the trees, in the hedges, among the flower-beds and potato-voyers, little filaments of green, little knobs of brown, were pushing forth. Gradually the subtle influence of the season came over Paul and mastered him, and as once before in the presence of the sea, so now again he fell into a waking dream. Now it was no alien monster that cast its spell over him, but the kindly familiar earth, mother and nurse of all living. Rush and leap as we will, we are like the apple trees, rooted deep in her ; when the sap rises in the elms it rises in us too ; we bud and burgeon with the thorn and the hazel. From her we come, to her we go. We are her children, she feeds us all our lives, and the happiest, healthiest of us are those that remain as it were babes unweaned, clinging to her breast, sucking life directly from her. Such are they that dig and plough, sow and reap, in fields and gardens.

With vacant eyes Paul stood, and felt the spring stir around him, within him too. The upward push of blade and tendril could almost be seen ; one was ready to fancy one could hear the rustling of the root fibres below, as they struggled through the earth, spreading their fine nets to catch moist nourishment. There stood the apple trees, a grey weather-beaten company. To a touch their trunks were cold, to a push they were stubbornly motionless, as dead things. But they lived, grew, had offspring, and died after fulfilment, like men. They had their troubles and struggles too ; every knot, every twist and angle of their branches told a tale of battle. They shrank from wind and cold, they groped after warmth and light, children of earth, brothers in sympathy and origin to men. They felt, they suffered and rejoiced ; blind, deaf, speechless, incapable of locomotion, they lived a life of the nature of which we can have no conception ; but they lived. Who knows but that they might hold some dim communion with other dumb things, with sun and air, with rain, with insects and birds? With each other, perhaps, tossing odours across and back, rubbing twig on twig, the friendly wind their go-between. The wind blew ; they leapt a scale in creation, and became creatures of lively motion. The wind was their soul, dwelling outside their bodies, like the soul of the giant in the fairy tale.

The earth is not as the sea, there is no treachery in her. The corn is faithful, it grows where it is planted. The trees pledge their word with flowers and fulfil it with fruit. Lend the soil seed, it repays it duly with interest. The fisherman gambles on his green cloth, the farmer banks his labour. One fights a fierce enemy, the other works shoulder to shoulder with a trusted friend. A happy life, and surely not a dull one, with green miracles working round one all the year, oneself the miracle-monger.

Did Paul's thoughts run so, as he leaned and stared across the garden, till the earth seemed to heave with thick life beneath his eyes? His visionary mood ran in thrills of feeling rather than in thoughts, thrills hardly to be translated into words, even by one more skilled in self-observation than he. The spell of the earth-magic held him. Jennifer had to call him twice before he awoke and remembered breakfast.

As he ate, ideas began to ferment. The riotous sap of spring was in his veins, impelling him to be up and doing. The garden dragged him to itself with every fibre, beckoned with every unfolding tendril. How if he did a little digging, to work off superfluous energy and pass the time away? So he would. Fine sport, gardening—calling for much craft and judgment; for muscle too. Better than muck-ing about with gashly, slimy fish. Fish! he was sick of fish. What did Jennifer suppose might be the price of land hereabouts? Which was considered the best soil? And where was the spade?

N

To think that the garden had lain before his eyes all this while, and he had never seen it, as one may say! And if there was an occupation after his own heart, an occupation he had pined to indulge in from his earliest youth, it was digging.

Naturally, everybody's fortune was as good as made. The garden was a tidy li'll splat o' ground, big enough for a family concern, so to speak, but no better than a jumping-off place for Pauline ambition. However, one could make a start with it; the field could be rented in the autumn say, and the farm next year. Meanwhile we have our eyes on a nice li'll blog of a horse; when we have time we will hunt about for a market cart. Let the Lanwiddock greengrocer shake in his shoes; his custom is as good as gone already. Broc'lo, early potatoes, onions, rhubarb, punkins—yes, to be sure, punkins!—no soil like Cornish soil for them all. Would Jennifer mind running over to the cove and fetching Dummy? Paul hadn't time. The breakfast things? She could wash them up afterwards. While she was there she might go into the shop and buy a spade—two spades. Her father might like to do some digging too. She might do some herself; 'twas splendid healthy exercise, and she had been looking wisht and pale this long time past.

Before her shawl was over her head he had hunted up a spade and was digging furiously. When she returned with Dummy there was already a dark line of freshly-turned mould scored across the garden from hedge to hedge, and Paul, axe in hand, was in the act of demolishing an ancient apple tree that stood solitary, apart from its fellows, in the middle of the plot. 'Twas only an incumbrance, long past bearing, good for firewood and nothing else. He was going to make a clean sweep, dig everything up and start afresh on virgin soil. Dig, Dummy! Dig, Jennifer! There was an easy bit of ground over there by the hedge, cram full of weeds and rubbishing flowers, a positive eyesore. Jennifer might begin there at once. What was she hesitating about? He had picked out an easy bit on purpose, and she could stop whenever she felt tired.

Mr Jose, coming home towards midday, rubbed his eyes and gaped at the sudden transformation wrought in his li'll splat o' ground. The apple tree laid flat, the soil all turned up, Paul, Dummy, and Jennifer digging away for dear life in three separate corners—what did it all mean?

Paul waved him in, helped him off with his coat, and thrust a hoe into his hands before he knew where he was. A dazzling, glowing account of the latest scheme left him gasping, more than half convinced of its plausibility. In dazed obedience to Paul's urgent summons he dealt the ground a few feeble pecks with the hoe. Then he straightened himself and tried to recover breath.

'What a chap!' he murmured.

His eyes fell on Jennifer. He started, and uttered an exclamation.

'Why, Jennifer, what are 'ee up to, rootin' up your flower-bed? Such a wan as you are for flowers, too! I never see a prettier show than you had last summer-time : an' no wonder, wi' the trouble you took, teelin' et an' waterin' et. An' now you've gone and dug et all up!'

'Why, law me!' exclaimed Paul remorsefully. 'I tauld her to dig there myself. I dedn' knaw; she never said nothin'. Thou fullish maid, Jennifer, how dedn' 'ee tell me? I dedn' look to spoil your pleasure like that.'

Jennifer was blushing.

'Edn' no consequence,' she murmured

shamefacedly. 'I don't belong to set so much store by them as I ded.'

'An' you're right!' exclaimed Paul. 'They're poor truck, flowers are—no use to nobody; only a vain show, cumberin' the ground.' The phrase took his fancy; like Browning's thrush, and for the same reason, he repeated it. 'A vain show, cumberin' the ground. You med as well fit an' teel thistles an' dralyers to wance. Weeds weth a grand name—that's all they are. There's a brave row of onions springin' up in my head along there, Jennifer. Better'n scroffy gilliflowers an' butter-'n-eggs, aha!'

'Ess, to be sure they are,' said Jennifer.

Mr Jose stared at his daughter.

'Such a wan as you were for flowers!' he muttered, shaking his head. He didn't understand the maid at all of late. Was it weak health, or mere flightiness?

In the afternoon there were curious faces peeping over the garden wall at the excavators. Reports of the digging operations had reached Porthvean, and a rumour spread that buried treasure had been found in Ben Jose's garden. It revived a flicker of the old amused amazement at Paul's doings, which quickly died away when it was discovered that he was embarking on nothing more out of the common than a little gardening. There was nothing in that. Every man among them had his plot of ground, snuggled away in a sheltered corner by the stream, or perched among boulders on the steep cliff-side; and there he teeled his potatoes and cabbages on windy days— modestly, be it understood, as one pursuing a private pastime; not making a misleading parade of it before the world, hallooing, flourishing one's spade, digging with the desperate energy of a gold-miner, betraying one's neighbours into a display of weak curiosity. Going to make his fortune by it, no doubt. Yah! Cod-liver oil! Going to drop fishing in favour of the new fad? So the rumour runs, but it fails to placate us. The head and front of the offending may be removed, but the rancour remains, too deeply seated to be easily brushed away. We are honest folks all, but . we could tolerate a rogue among us, if by fair means or foul he would rid us of this ramping, roaring nuisance.

CHAPTER XV

HE SUFFERS A CHECK

HAMPERED by the smallest possible modicum of experience, Paul dug and sowed zealously for a fortnight. The potatoes were in, and the onions, the cauliflowers, carrots, beans, and so on through the list. We are nothing if not thorough; every esculent vegetable must be represented. Pumpkin seed was not to be had, but vegetable marrow would do as well. Better; was it not a native product, and so superior to aught that the Yankees could show? Let Jennifer wait till she tasted it, baked in a pie with a few drops of essence of lemon for flavouring. Even in Cornwall, land of pies and pasties, there was nothing like it; let her take Paul's word for that.

Suddenly, in the midst of his operations, Paul suffered a rude check. His pockets were found to be empty. What with tools and seeds, not ten shillings remained of his little store. And there was no immediate prospect of replenishment, either. After all, in one respect agriculture compares unfavourably with fishing: the returns are heart-rendingly slow. Months to wait before a farthing comes back, and nothing to do all the time but a little paltry weeding and training. Not even a Paul Carah can conquer the deliberation of Mother Earth. Personal magnetism avails nothing with a voyer of potatoes, and no amount of hustling will compel onions to work double tides. After all, there was a good deal to be said for fishing, especially for crabbing, which had all the charm of an untried novelty. And what was this in his ears? The echo of a sneering chuckle, of a derisive insinuation that he had lost heart, that Porthvean's black looks were too much for him, that he was about to throw up his hand and retire defeated? The spades were thrown into a corner, out came pots and brushes, and off hied Paul post-haste to paint his boat.

The crab-pots, as has been said, were piled in the out-house where their manufacture had been carried on. And there also the other gear was stored for the time, having been brought over from the fish-cellar by the quay to be repaired at leisure. Now they must be moved back. When the painting and tarring of the boat was completed, he and Dummy started on the pots. Pots are bulky things, and heavier than one would think, to look at them. Working through the afternoon and into the darkness of the evening, there were still some pots—a dozen or so—remaining in the out-house, and the other gear had not been touched. 'Twas tiring work, and they left the rest for next day. Paul was fagged out, and whether he secured the out-house door or no, he cannot remember. He came in, ordered his supper at once, bolted it, and stumbled up to bed, where he slept, as he always slept, soundly and dreamlessly until the morning. Jennifer's slumbers were more disturbed : she slept lightly of late. She dreamt she was in the garden, chopping up the old apple tree into fire-wood; and in the small hours she awoke with a start, with a dream-echo of retreating footsteps in her ears. She listened, but heard nothing, and presently fell asleep again.

In the morning, after breakfast, Paul went to the out-house, meaning to carry two or three

pots with him as he went over to the cove to
rouse Dummy, who was apt to be lazy of a
morning. He threw open the door, made one
step within, and stood aghast. The pots
which the night before he had left safely
stacked in a corner, were lying strewn about
the floor in a state of hopeless wreck. Some
were mere heaps of twigs; all had been
hacked and smashed—with an axe apparently—
in a way to render them quite useless and beyond repair.

Paul's shout of infuriate amazement brought
Jennifer out. The sight of the destruction
shook her composure, and she screamed. The
shock had stunned Paul, and he stood staring
stupidly, his hands relaxed and aimlessly
groping. She caught one in her own and held
it firmly ; and so they remained for a while.

Paul began to recover ; his eyes went about
the shed, seeking a clue. Suddenly he snatched
his hand from Jennifer's—indeed, he had never
noticed her action or felt her grasp—and darted
forward.

'The gear!' he cried. ''Tes gone!'

The nets and lines should have been hanging
by nails on the wall ; but it was as Paul said,
their place was vacant. He hunted desperately

in every corner; they were not to be found. Then he rushed blindly from the shed, vaulted the gate, and pelted towards the cove, shouting his loss as he went.

By the quay he ran into a peacefully chatting group—ran right through them, scattering them in all directions. He pulled up, and turned on them, foaming and panting.

'Rogues!' he shouted. 'Rogues an' robbers! Where's my gear? Fetch en out, before I smash the lot of 'ee.'

They growled ominously, and closed up together, like sheep before a barking cur.

'Look!' came a voice from a safe position in the rear. 'Look, Paul Carah; we haven't a notion what you're a-tellin' of, but we edn' to be spoke of in that way. We're nothin' but dirt in the sight of 'ee, no doubt, but—'

The orator stopped perforce. Paul had darted off as abruptly as he had arrived, making for the fish-cellars, and fumbling in his pocket as he went. The remaining pots—had the rogues got at them too?

There were marks of hard usage on the cellar door, but it was safely locked. He pulled out the key, and unlocked it. Thank goodness, they were all there, intact and undisturbed. He hurried back.

'Thank 'ee for not smashin' the cellar door! But where's my gear, you pack o' thieves? Where's et to?'

The orator resumed his spoilt flight of eloquence.

'I've no doubt we're nothin' but dirt—'

'Nor I nuther, but that edn' the question. Where's my gear?'

Another voice arose, a voice of oily regret.

'Vexed to say we don't none of us knaw, Paul. But ef I might give a guess, maybe you've fit an' buried et in your sleep, seein' that your mind's that set on diggin' jus' now.'

We are in no laughing humour, but Jim Boase's utterances must be honoured in the customary way.

Paul glared round, hungry for a fight, uncertain which rogue to pitch on among so many. One face he sought for, but it was missing.

'Steve! He's hidin', of course. An' you d' all knaw why. Aw, you're a virtuous lot, 'specially when there's a drunken rogue handy to do your dirty work for 'ee! Where's Steve?'

"'Whoever 'a es, I'll find en out 'fore long,' he cried."

'Come now!' exclaimed Jim Boase in tones of pained reproach. 'See what unjust be-'aviour anger do lead 'ee into. Steve went off yes'day mornin' to Falmouth on an arrand for Reseigh, an' he edn' back yet.'

Paul's wrath hung ·suspended, caught in a net of bewilderment. He had instinctively, inevitably pitched on Steve as the actual culprit; and here were his accomplices ready with an alleged alibi. They were all tarred with the same brush; one stood out among them adorned with an extra coating, satanically black; if he wriggled from one's grasp, whom among the rest, uniform in their dingy knavery, could one fix upon? Baffled, he turned away.

'Whoever 'a es, I'll find en out 'fore long,' he called over his shoulder. 'Trust me. I'm an honest man, but I've all the wits of a rogue. An' don't ye look to drive me out this way. Profanin' dedn' do et; laffin' dedn' do et; an' thievin' waan't do et nuther. An' so for you.'

What to do now he hardly knew. Automatically he turned homeward, the hot blood in him driving him along at top speed. At first, rage continued to hold him, to the exclusion of all else; but gradually the steady swing of leg and arm did its soothing, clarifying work; and he began to think with a brain comparatively calm.

'Twas ruin, or something near it. True, the boat remained, and two-thirds of the fleet of pots. But for two months yet they would scarcely earn their up-keep in bait, and how was the lost gear to be replaced when he had no money left? Replaced it must be, and at once, if he was to continue the fight. Oh, 'twas hard! He had worked as no man had ever worked before; he had knowingly offended no man; he had gone out of his way to please; and this was the upshot—empty pockets, the imminent prospect of debt, and a town full of foes.

The thief might be caught yet, and the stolen gear recovered. A difficult task, with no clue visible, and one net or line as like another as peascod to peascod. Still, with craft and unremitting watchfulness. . . .

He walked faster and thought deeper. Within the cottage he found Mr Jose and Jennifer talking together. With sympathy for fuel his wrath flared out anew. Porthvean was rotten with roguery from end to end. It was drenched in crime, like shavings in paraffin. No place for the good man, ever carrying the naked lamp of honesty to guide him in the straight path.

He had a jealous thought 'twas Steve after all, in spite of his ostentatious alibi. He was the biggest rogue ; he had been head and chief against Paul all the while.

Mr Jose agreed, but angered Paul by trotting out his ancient prejudice against Reseigh. The plan wasn't cunning enough for Steve, he said. The hand of a craftier villain was apparent. Steve's soul wasn't his own ; he was Reseigh's tool. It was on an errand of Reseigh's that Steve was ostensibly absent, wasn't it ? Well then !

Paul fretted. This prejudice against Reseigh was unaccountable. If he had dark designs against Paul, what were they ? And how was his unremitting friendliness to be accounted for ?

Mr Jose did not pretend to fathom the depths of Reseigh's villainy ; that was beyond him. But this he knew: there was not enough kindly feeling in the shopkeeper to fill a thimble. If he paraded friendship for a man, 'twas for his own ends. There was no human feeling in him save the lust of power and gold. He was nothing but a great, cruel, bloated spider.

He had all Porthvean in his web, sucking their blood; before Paul knew it, the viscous net would be about him; and then struggle as he might, he would never be free.   Why, look! there was Billy Drew, as fine a young fellow as ever you met.   Billy got married, and borrowed ten pounds of Reseigh on the strength of it.   In five years he paid back fifty, and still the ten pounds remained miraculously undiminished.   Then Billy kicked.   He abused Reseigh to his face, and refused to pay another farthing.   What was the result?   Billy was sold up, stock, lock and barrel, and left Porth-vean penniless.

And of whom was this fable narrated, Paul wanted to know?   He wasn't going to get married; no such fool.   If Reseigh found another man's hand under his heel, small blame to him if he stamped on it.   And a truce to this slanderous backbiting of a worthy man, a true friend, if there ever was one.

Now, listen.   Paul had a plan.   A secret invocation of the strong arm of the law; a sudden descent of the police on all the cellars and attics in Porthvean; nets and lines captured, and a rogue marched off to prison. What did Ben Jose think of that, aha?

Ben Jose had cold water ready. The arm of the law, *videlicet*, the Lanwiddock policeman, was a poor weapon for prompt action. He was five miles off, to begin with. Moreover, he was a peaceable man, and had never arrested a criminal in his life. Serving an occasional writ was as far as he had gone. Beloved of all the country-side, he took care to do nothing to endanger his popularity and disturb his life of ease. Police in Porthvean! Mr Jose sympathised deeply with Paul, but the credit of his native village counted for something, and the idea of employing such drastic measures took his breath away. Anything rather than that!

What then? Eight pounds' worth of gear gone, the season at hand, and no money in Paul's pockets. If ever a situation called for drastic measures it was this.

Jennifer made a sign to her father.

'Eh!' he exclaimed. 'Aw ess, to be sure. Look 'ee here, sonny,' he said to Paul; 'Jennifer an' me have been talkin' while you were away, an' Jennifer, she thinks—'

He stopped, at another vehement sign from his daughter.

'Aw ess, I forgot,' he stammered on

o

'Edn' no consarn o' Jennifer's. But we were talkin', as I say, an' I was tellin' Jennifer how I thought maybe, seein' as how we're all friendly like, an' you bein' wan o' the family, so to spake, or gettin' on that way—Hauld on, Jennifer, you put me all in a maze, interruptin' like that—you bein' wan o' the family, as I say, I thought maybe you wouldn' take offence ef we trated you *as* wan o' the family : an' so— an' so ef eight pound, or maybe ten, 'ull be of any sarvice ti' 'ee, why, 'tes *at* your sarvice, so to spake.'

The good man mopped his brow and looked expectantly at Paul. Jennifer's eyes were in her lap.

'Uncle,' said Paul coldly, 'I can see you don't mane no offence, so I don't take none. Nor I don't take no money nuther. I edn' a beggar yet, nor my stomach edn' empty 'nough to hauld no charity. I stand on my own feet, ef you plaise, an' I pay my own way so long as I'm able, an' owe no man a halfpenny.'

'But 'a edn' a loan I do offer 'ee ; 'tes a gift, a friendly gift,' cried Mr Jose eagerly.

'Money or thanks, 'tes all the same,' Paul replied. ' I owe them to no man. I stand on my own feet.'

'Twas a sublime attitude, and he knew it. The old fellow looked sufficiently uncomfortable and humiliated. How did Jennifer take it? Her eyes were in her lap.

'There, don't say no more about et,' he exclaimed generously. 'I forgive 'ee. You don't understand my natur' yet. I edn' like other men. I waan't say I'm better, nor I waan't say I'm worse; I'm defferent, that's all. Ask me a favour, I'm thankful. Offer me a gift, I'm vexed. That's me.'

Surely a loftier peak of virtue was never trodden by mortal foot. Wrapt in ecstatic self-contemplation, he forgot his troubles. What a noble fellow he was, to be sure, with his sturdy independence, his scorn of gold! He could see the timid admiration in the old man's eyes. And Jennifer, what did she think?

'Edn' I right, Jennifer, to stand on my own feet an' take help from no man? Edn' I right?'

She lifted her eyes. What queer eyes they were, to be sure! Their intensity stabbed one.

'Ess, Paul, you're right,' she murmured sadly.

'Why, Jennifer!' exclaimed her father. ''Twas you yourself—'

'What's that?' asked Paul, as the old man stopped abruptly.

'Nothin',' he replied, staring at Jennifer in some alarm.

Paul followed his eyes.

'Jennifer,' he said, 'you're lookin' wisht, sim' me. Bustle about an' do some churrs. 'A edn' healthy for a g'eat maid like you to sit idle. Bustle, now, while me an' your da talk over this here business. You women d' 'ave an easy time of et; all the trouble an' worry goes to the men. Woman's life—churrs an' chatter, that's about et; arter that you're no manner o' use. Come, bustle!'

CHAPTER XVI

HE WALKS INTO THE PARLOUR

RESEIGH, enjoying the evening air at the shop door, saw Paul hurrying up the street, and beckoned to him as he passed. 'Step inside, Paul,' he said. 'I was lookin' out for 'ee. Step inside an' have a chat with an auld fellow.'

Paul followed him into the musty shop. Two of the village wives, at voluble argument with the girl over the counter, came to a sudden silence as the two entered, and stared curiously at Paul.

'Are 'ee sarved yet, Mis' Jackson an' Mis' Polsue?' asked the master.

'Ess, to be sure,' said Mrs Jackson, with hurried obsequiousness. 'Haelf a pound o' candles an' a pennord o' saffern.'

'Happord o' pins an' happord o' sugar,' added Mrs Polsue.

'An' sixpennord o' scand'lous gossip, I've
no doubt,' said Reseigh.

They laughed nervously.

'On'y havin' a bit of a chat,' apologised
Mrs Jackson.

'Finished yet?'

'Ess, s'pose.'

'Paid?'

'Well, no. We thought you wouldn' mind
us trustin' 'ee a bit longer.'

'Entered?' This to the girl.

'Just a-goin' to,' she replied in a terrified
voice.

'Gossip first, business afterwards. That's
your way, is 'a? Gie me the book.'

He opened the bulky register of Porthvean's
woes, turned over some leaves, and made the
entries.

'I'll divide the sixpennord o' gossip between
'ee—thruppence aich,' he said, and wrote again,
without a chuckle at his grim joke.

They quavered a laugh, not daring to protest.
He shut the book with a bang.

'An' now, out wi' 'ee, quick. I pay the maid
to work, not to chatter with auld go-'bouts.
Out you go.'

They scuttled off, and Reseigh turned to the girl.

'You're a fine one,' he said. 'Put up the shutters, an' go thee'st home. I waste no words on 'ee, but you'd better be'ave.'

His manner changed as he turned and addressed Paul.

'Will 'ee walk into my parlour, Paul?'

What obscure memory was it that jingled at the back of Paul's brain? And why, at that particular moment, should he be thinking of Ben Jose's lurid comparison of Reseigh to a spider?

They entered the little back room, Reseigh carefully closing the door behind him.

'Sit down, Paul,' he said, 'an' make yourself comfortable.'

He sat down himself, facing Paul.

'Paul,' he said, 'I hear you're in trouble, an' vexed I am to hear et.'

The flood-gates were opened, the torrent poured forth. Reseigh listened politely, with a grave 'Well, well!' or 'Scand'lous!' where occasion demanded, until the whole iniquity of Porthvean had been laid bare.

'A bad business,' said Reseigh, when Paul had shouted himself into the temporary silence of breathlessness. 'A bad business, sure 'nough. I wouldn' ha' b'lieved et o' Porthvean folk, though I haven' much opinion of 'em, nuther.'

A sensible chap, this. He and Paul were of one mind there.

'When a chap's in trouble,' continued Reseigh, 'then's the time for his true friends to show themselves.'

A frown began to gather on Paul's face. Was another insulting proposal coming? Reseigh's eyes on him were the cat's on the suspicious sparrow.

'D'ye mind,' he said, 'what I tauld 'ee when you come here first? They were agin you then, an' I said ti' 'ee, said I—"You're welcome to anythin' in my shop, an' pay when you like." You mind that, don't you?'

Paul did, and his frown darkened. If Reseigh thought—

A wave of Reseigh's hand stopped him.

'That was before I understood your char'cter. I dedn' knaw you then—your pardon for that. I knaw you now, an' I wouldn' make no such offer, not for worlds. Help? You edn' the sort that looks for help. You stand on your own feet, you do.'

His own words! Inevitably he thought of a scene lately transacted in the Joses' cottage, and the contrast shed a blaze of glory on Reseigh's head.   Here, at least, was one who understood and admired him.

'Ef 'twas another chap, an' I liked him as I've growed to like you, my hand 'ud be in my pocket to wance.   You've heard hard words agin me in the town, I've no doubt, but I edn' what they do want to make me out.   They don't understand my char'cter, no more than they do yours.   I'm fo'ced to sim hard to the world, or the world 'ud stank me under ets heel. But my natur' edn' so.'

That was what Paul was always telling them. A kinder-hearted, more generous fellow than Reseigh did not exist.   Paul had always stuck up for him, and always would.   Misunderstood, grossly vilified, they were a pair; 'twas their duty to stand shoulder to shoulder.

Reseigh was very grateful to Paul for his kind words; and it *was* their duty, as Paul said, to stand shoulder to shoulder.

'Well,' he continued, 'ef 'twas any other chap but you, as I said, I'd offer 'ee my shop an' my purse, an' be proud for 'ee to take what you liked.   Seein' et's you, I don't.   But

I've an offer to make 'ee, f'rall that. Edn' no
question o' help. 'Tes what you may call
mutual 'ccommodation—a kind o' partnership,
you may say.'

Paul was all gratified attention.

'I've got a scheme,' Reseigh went on;
'an' 'tes a scheme that wants a bauld, active,
crafty chap to carr' en out.'

A scheme? Paul pricked up his ears.

'"Where am I to find such a chap?" said I;
an' I looked round, an' there wadn' none. Then
you came; an' soon's I clapped eyes upon 'ee
—"That's the chap for me!" said I. "Ef I
could pick the world over, that's the chap."
Well, I'm slow an' careful, so I watched 'ee an'
watched 'ee, makin' my plans the while; an'
now they're ready, an' I'm ready, an' sim' me
you're ready too, ef you'll agree.'

Bold, active—we are ready for anything.
Crafty—we do not commit ourselves rashly,
but wait for further particulars.

'You smoke a pipe,' said Reseigh, 'so you
d' knaw how cheap an' good I sell tobacco.
You don't drink—you're too sensible for that—
but you've noticed what a lot o' little-drop men
there are in this town. An' how? Brandy's
cheap over to "Fisherman's Arms." Cheap

tobacco an' cheap brandy; spell that out for
me.'

Paul winked knowingly. *He* knew well
enough.

"'Course you do. Chap goes out from here
to draw his nets. French trawler comes along.
" Got any fish?" says he. " Ess, plenty o' fish."
"We want fish?" says Frenchy. "You want
tabac, odyvee?" Our chap nods his head.
They draw up alongside; our chap throws up
the fish, Frenchy lowers a keg or a package, as
the case may be, an' so good-bye. Keg or
package, et comes to me; I don't knaw where
'a comes from, nor I don't ask; 'tes offered
cheap, an' I buy et.

' Well, you say, edn' nothin' out o' the common in that; 'tes the same all round the coast.
'Tes in the blood of us Cornishmen. But 'tes a
mean business nowadays, not like what 'a was
in the auld ancient time. Why, there edn' a house
in Porthvean, nor a farm up-country for miles,
that hasn' got its secret hidin'-places under
drexles an' between planchin's an' inside roofs,
where they used to keep the stuff. In this very
house—but I'll show 'ee presently. They were
all in et—bauld Cornishmen, wan an' all, an' a
fig for English preventives! The sperit's clane

gone out of 'em now.   Time to wake et up agin,
say I, an' bring the auld days back.'

He stooped and glanced at Paul's eager face,
snuffing romantic adventure.   His eyes nar-
rowed, and he stretched out a fat hand and laid
it on Paul's arm.

'You're the wan to do et,' he said.
'Young, bauld, crafty, you're the wan.'

So he was!   Reseigh's words were the bugle
to the war-horse, sounding the charge.   Every
fibre in him responded.   Patriotism, adventurous risk, scope for scheming, dazzling prospect of fortune—was ever venture so completely
congenial?

'Now look,' continued Reseigh. 'I'm
auld an' fat; my brain edn' like yourn; 'tes
slow an' dull.   But I've worked out a sort of a
plan in my slow, tayjous way, an' 'tes at your
sarvice ef you like to hear en.'

By all means.   Out with the little plan, and
we'll do our best to lick it into shape.

Humbly inviting criticism, Reseigh proceeded
to explain.   In the way of business, he had
correspondence with a certain fish-buyer, who
also owned some boats, in a certain town on
the coast of Brittany.   Arrangements might be
made—in fact, they had already been made in

a tentative fashion—by which, on occasions depending on the state of moon and tide, a boat belonging to his correspondent would sail on a trawling expedition across Channel. With a full cargo, and the Breton coast far away, what more natural than that it should make for Pendennack or Porthloy, there to dispose of its fish? On its way, 'twould be easy to reach a prearranged spot outside Porthvean at a prearranged time; a spot where a Porthvean man might have set his lines or nets without exciting the least suspicion. If the Porthvean man happened to be there at the prearranged time, attending to his lines, it seemed likely that the boats would run across each other; and if the French boat had more of what we will call ' ballast' on board than was convenient, it might conceivably choose that moment to chuck it overboard. Contrary to the habits of ordinary ballast, it would float, being attached to an empty barrel, or what not. The Porthvean man's interest would be aroused at this singular phenomenon, and when the French boat had sailed away, he would row up and haul the innocent bit of flotsam on board, there to investigate at his leisure. The curious discovery he would then make would induce him to hoist his sail and return, to communicate it to Reseigh. What did Paul think of that ?

Paul was delighted. The manœuvre by which the necessity of actual communication between the craft was obviated, was a stroke of genius, worthy of his own brain. A tidy li'll plan, sure 'nough. But his present function was criticism. The coastguard : how about them ? Risk he gloried in ; he wasn't the one to shirk *that*. But daring should go hand in hand with caution. Any fool could blunder into danger. Here were the coastguard ; he snapped his fingers at them, but here they were. Bravery was one thing, foolhardiness another ; and landing kegs on quay-head under the nose of the look-out man seemed to come under the latter category.

Paul was implored to listen for a bit. The coastguardsmen were not so formidable as he imagined. To begin with, the very boldness of the scheme, running the contraband right under their noses, was calculated to disarm suspicion. Besides, individually the men were disposed to be friendly. The married ones mostly had their little accounts running at Reseigh's shop, same as everybody else in the village. Reseigh kept the amount well before their eyes, but never pressed too keenly for payment, knowing what a struggle the poor chaps had to keep their families respectably clothed on the Government pittance. As for the single men, maybe they appreciated the merits of cheap tobacco and grog as well as anybody else. Married or single, they had a corner in their hearts for Reseigh, and they would not see more than they were forced to see. Still, Paul was right, sharp-witted fellow that he was ; one must not obtrudé one's little affairs on official notice. He had hit on the crux, too— the conveyance of the goods from the boat to the shore. Now, if Paul wouldn't mind getting up and following, he would show him something.

Reseigh lit a candle, and preceded Paul out of the parlour into the shop, and thence by another way into a passage. At the end of the passage was a door which opened directly on a flight of steps leading cellarwards. At the bottom, another door, which had to be unlocked. Passing through this, they were in a spacious cellar, piled to the ceiling with Reseigh's reserve stock of goods — barrels of flour and petroleum, bales of calico, cases of tinned meat, and the like. Paul stared curiously about him.

'Where d'ye s'pose we are now?' said Reseigh.

'Underground, s'pose,' said Paul.

'Ess, we're that; an' above ground too. There's a c'numdrum for 'ee. Underground an' above ground too — what d'ye make o' that?'

Paul could make nothing of it.

'Come, now,' Reseigh prompted. 'Where's my shop? On the clift, edn' 'a? Where's this cellar then?'

'I mind 'ee now! 'Tes inside the clift, like-a-thing,' cried Paul, delighted at his own acuteness.

''Course 'a es,' said Reseigh approvingly. 'An' bein' so, 'tes underground an' overground, as I said—under the road an' over the cove. Look 'ee here. Lend a hand wi' this barr'l.'

It stood at the further end of the cellar, in a kind of recess. When it was rolled away, a blank wall of rough-hewn granite appeared.

'Now,' said Reseigh, 'what's the clift like, under my shop, lookin' from quay-head?'

Paul recalled its appearance. It rose sheer from the water, and it was faced with granite blocks, to prevent it from crumbling away.

'Very well. Now cast your eye on this

stone.' He indicated what was apparently a big block of granite, the size of a cottage window, set back a little from its fellows.

'Looks all right, don't 'a? Now watch.'

His hand groped at the side; his fingers disappeared into a crevice in the masonry; he tugged, and a sudden flood of moonlight poured on their faces. The seeming block was a thin slab, no thicker than a shutter, and like a shutter it had swung out of the wall at Reseigh's touch.

Paul uttered a cry of astonishment, and thrust his head through the opening. There below him lay the cove and the deserted quay, black against a background of silver moonlit sea.

'My nerves!' His head popped back, like a cork from a bottle, and he began to examine the artful contrivance with professional interest.

'My nerves!' He was a mason himself, but in all his experience he had never seen the like.

'Smart chaps in the auld days, wadn' they?' said Reseigh. 'You d' see the fashion of en? Cargo expected; man up here waitin'; hears a signal; opens, an' drops a rope with a grapnel 'pon the end. Men in the boat below make the

P

goods fast; man above hauls up, pushes the stone to, an' there edn' nothin' to be seen but an empty wall.'

Reseigh carefully closed the opening, turned to Paul, and looked him full in the face. Paul's eyes were glittering, and his whole demeanour expressed the liveliest excitement and fascination.

'Now,' said Reseigh, 'what d'ye say? Will 'ee join me?'

Would a cat eat cream?

'Shake han's, partner!' he shouted. ''Tes a bargain!'

Reseigh's cold flabby hand was wrung as it had never been wrung before. Then the barrel was rolled back, and they returned to the shop. It was growing late, and further discussion was postponed by mutual agreement. Paul prepared to depart. Just as he was going Reseigh called him back.

'Your gear,' he said. 'You must have some, an' I work et out like this. Seein' we're partners in the same boat, like, workin' together, there edn' no objection to me supplyin' the tayckle, is there? You'll need it for this li'll business of ourn.'

Of course. Things were on a different footing now, and Paul readily accepted Reseigh's kind offer.

'Edn' no sale, so edn' no debt,' said Reseigh. 'But et vexes me ef my stock don't tally with my books. 'Tes a wakeness o' mine. So I'll put en down in a reg'lar way, as ef '*twas* a debt, just as a matter o' form, an' cross et out arterwards, when the profits come in. You agree to that, don't 'ee?'

Paul agreed. He was always ready to humour a friend's weakness; and he was too full of other things to parley about a trivial matter casually mentioned in a matter-of-fact way. And so good-night to his dear friend and partner.

Paul strode off, and Reseigh locked the shop door and returned to the parlour, clucking softly with his tongue against the roof of his mouth. He never laughed spontaneously, but on the rare occasions when amusement called for expression, he was in the habit of making this clucking sound.

CHAPTER XVII

HE MAKES AN EXPEDITION

BEFORE parting, Reseigh had exacted a pledge of secrecy from Paul; and faithfully Paul kept it, after his own fashion. That is to say, he made no definite statement of fact; but his conversation fairly bristled with mysterious hints. He could talk of nothing else but the ancient glories of Cornwall, secret hiding-places, smuggled goods, short cuts to fortune, and the amiable and virtuous Reseigh. Directly questioned, he winked and grinned, begging them not to press him to reveal business secrets. Jennifer, who, in spite of the submissive dulness which had come over her, seemed never to let Paul's least word or action escape her notice, found it only too easy to piece his hints together, and read in them a meaning which filled her with apprehension. And then a brand new set of lines and nets appeared on the scene. Paul would offer no explanation of the portent, but it could only be interpreted in one way, by reference to that source of all evil, that nightmare oppressor of Porthvean's imagination, the big black book on Reseigh's counter. She saw spectral misfortune creeping up behind Paul's back, while he, frank, careless fellow, stamped and elbowed his way along, scornful of danger. Her heart cried out a warning to him, which her lips would not, could not, utter. For a while she suffered in silence, till solitary anxiety grew intolerable, and she confided her fears and suspicions to her father. He, worthy man, was seriously concerned, and felt it his duty, unpleasant enough with the memory of frequent rebuffs still fresh, to take Paul aside and add one more to his oft-repeated warnings against his bugbear, Reseigh. One result was inevitable—an explosion of wrath on Paul's part, and an indignant request that Ben Jose would mind his own business and leave others to mind theirs. There were other consequences. One was, that Paul's acumen being called into question, he threw his vow of secrecy—somewhat tattered already—to the winds, and confirmed every suspicion by boastfully proclaiming the name

and nature of the new scheme. Another
was that Jennifer being absent from the inter-
view, the old man blunderingly introduced her
name, not seeking thereby to avoid responsibility or shift the blame to her shoulders, but
wishing to emphasise his warning by showing
that another shared his fears. A third result
followed this. Paul, who was in a highly
nervous, excited state, sought Jennifer out, and
overwhelmed her with reproaches. In truth he
forgot himself so far as to grow abusive. She
was a meddlesome, interfering maid, like all
her tribe. Women! they were nothing but a
curse, sticking their fingers into every pie.
What right had she to pry into his business?
'Twas she, then, who had egged her father on
to pester and insult him with croaking words
of warning. Well, he had had enough of it,
let her understand that; he didn't put the
value of a snap of the fingers on a silly maid's
notions. If she wanted to burst the scheme and
ruin his fortune, let her put on her shawl and
be off, there and then, to the coastguard station.
She was capable of that, he didn't doubt.

Red and white by turns, till the red failed to
come, she endured the lash with a passive
silence which only incensed him more. She

disdained to answer, did she? Friends, were
they? He flung her friendship in her face,
with an oath to follow.

Then she trembled to her feet, staring wildly
at him.

'Paul,' she whispered, 'you're killin' me!
I caan't bear—'

She broke off with a cry, and fled to her
room.

To do him justice, he was frankly ashamed
of himself the moment after, and Jennifer had
scarcely locked her door before he was outside,
urgently seeking the forgiveness the poor girl
was only too ready to accord. Peace was
soon restored. For a day or two Paul, striving
generously to make amends, behaved with unexampled gentleness and consideration; and
for a day or two Jennifer was more like the
quietly cheerful Jennifer of old than she had
been for a long time past.

Adopting for a moment Ben Jose's estimate
of Reseigh, and supposing him to be in truth a
crafty, far-seeing villain, one might be disposed
to wonder that he cared to admit an indiscreet
babbler to share a plan, the most essential part
of which was complete secrecy. But, on pursuing one's considerations on the same ima-

ginary lines, one would be inclined to do
more justice to Reseigh's cunning. The hostile
attitude of Porthvean, which, in spite of his
protestations, Reseigh had never done anything to mollify, effectually closed Paul's mouth
to all but Mr Jose and Jennifer, and these latter,
one may suppose, he could afford to despise for
an honest, inoffensive pair, whose lips were
sealed by their friendship for Paul. Only
Dummy remained; and Dummy was a neg-
ligible quantity, a mere piece of boat's furni-
ture, physically debarred from blabbing, and
conveniently ignorant of the nature and existence
of customs laws. The fact of his being Paul's
partner halved the risk. All this, of course, is
unjustifiable supposition.

There were frequent consultations between
Paul and Reseigh. Paul's wits, busy as ever,
evolved one or two cunning improvements,
calculated to make the plan work with perfect
smoothness; and Reseigh accepted the sug-
gestions with many expressions of admiration.
One was intended to obviate the danger of finding people about the quay when one returned
from an expedition. This was a point to be
considered, when boats were coming and going
at all hours. Now the store-pots were sunk in

shallow water, two or three hundred yards from quay-head. If Paul planted his pot some way apart from the others, and if, instead of bringing the goods directly ashore, he sank them by a line attached to a float, close by the side of it, he could safely leave them there till a convenient opportunity offered for landing them.

And there was another scheme, more ornamental than useful, perhaps, but still worth trying. On shore and on sea there would be prying eyes, watching his every movement. He was going to circumvent them, and have a bit of fun at the same time. In addition to the ordinary boat's lantern he intended to carry two others—a red one and a green one. A dark night, the red lantern in the bow, the green one in the stern—and there was your phantom steamer all complete. Now, suppose another boat inconveniently near at the critical moment. And suppose the occupants were suddenly to see, looming out of the darkness, a red light bearing straight down upon them: would they not get out of the way brave and quick, trembling, before the worst danger a fisherman has to face—the danger of being run down in the darkness? And suppose that, just as they caught sight of the second light, both red and green were suddenly extinguished, as if the supposed steamer had sunk like a stone. And let this happen not once only, but twice or thrice—what a fine tale of a spectre-ship could be made out of that! And what boat would venture after dark in the neighbourhood of the spot where the apparition had been seen?

It speaks volumes for Reseigh's simple faith in Paul's genius, that this plan, which another man might have deemed absurdly fantastical, met with his express approval. But, indeed, he never ventured to thwart or oppose Paul in any way—that is, in any visible way. Paul plumed himself, with apparent justice, on having the redoubtable arbiter of Porthvean's destinies completely under his thumb. Oh, 'twas grand to parade him up and down, like a tame bear, before the scowling wonder of the town! To march into the shop at the busiest time of the day, and with a beckoning finger, spirit him off into the private room, leaving an amazed, whispering crowd behind! Partners? 'Twas master and man, more like. This the subtle rogue of Ben Jose's imagination? Pouf! A meek, old dodderer, slow-witted, easily led, eager to please. And, mark you, a single man, wealthy, heirless, and without a spark of affection for any one but Paul. You take our meaning, aha! Golden dreams arise, dreams only as yet, but built, as few dreams are built, on a solid foundation of undeniable fact.

With the first few days of March the fishing began, in an irregular tentative way at first, till in a week or so the weather settled, and every net, line, and pot in Porthvean was in the water, earning money. The time had arrived for the great scheme to take practical shape. The lines were out at the appointed spot, the store-pot was cunningly sunk at a place invisible from the shore; one only awaited the waning of the moon and the letter with the foreign stamp.

The letter came; the expedition was made, and crowned with complete success. There was one critical moment, when Dummy, in the dim light of early dawn, saw a hole open in the harbour wall, and a face appear, white in a frame of dark stone. He fairly yelled with astonishment. The face disappeared, the opening was swiftly closed, and Paul had half an hour in which to abuse Dummy under his breath. Then, as it appeared that no sleepers had been awakened, the face showed again, and the rest of the job was safely and quickly transacted.

But at intervals during the day a farcical incident occurred and recurred on the quay. The actors were Paul and Dummy. Dummy would come down from the street, take his station midway along the quay, opposite the back windows of Reseigh's shop, and stare fascinated at the wall beneath, chattering loud astonishment, and gesticulating bewildered arguments with himself. A few minutes after, Paul would hurry down in an agony of apprehension, rate his partner soundly, and haul him away. In half-an-hour the mysterious fascination of the wall would draw Dummy back, and the scene would be repeated. About the third time of performance Porthvean began to be interested, slightly amused, and puzzled a good deal. Little knots gathered on the quay, dividing their attention between Dummy and the harbour wall. Then Paul grew frantic, and the fourth time he intercepted Dummy on his way down, ran him back to the fish-cellar, and, without further ado, locked him in.

There was one who was neither amused nor

puzzled.   Steve Polkinhorne, idly lounging
as usual on quay-head, saw the first performance of the little drama, pondered over it
briefly, and leapt to his feet with an oath.   He
ran along the quay, and, as he ran, he was
seen distinctly by two or three to shake his fist
at Reseigh's windows.   The next authentic
news of him reports him sitting in the bar of
the 'Fisherman's Arms,' in company with his
partner, John Trembath, drinking deeply, and
detailing in whispers some matter which seemed
to   incense   him   greatly.   With   successive
glasses his voice grew louder ;   fragments of
his talk were audible—fragments of rancorous
abuse directed against Paul, and not only
against Paul (there was nothing new in that),
but—oh portent !—against Reseigh himself—
Reseigh, to whom, as earthly representative
and agent of the Evil One, he had sold himself, body and soul.   The landlord of the inn—
nominally landlord, but really Reseigh's tenant
and humble servant—heard Reseigh's name
coupled with a bad word.   This was treason ;
it must to the master's ears.   He quietly put
on his hat and went over to the shop.   When
he returned he was closely followed by Reseigh,

who, without uttering a word, fixed his eyes on Steve and raised a sternly beckoning finger. The sight jumped Steve halfway back to sobriety. He stumbled to his feet and meekly followed Reseigh out of the bar. Later on he was observed slinking out of the shop, the very image of a beaten cur. Later still, for a period of days, he skulked and growled in corners, apprehension peeping from behind black wrath in his eyes.

To us, who do not care to tread the noisome crooked ways of a rogue's thoughts and motives, the meaning of all this is not easy to fathom; and we do not wish to undertake the unpleasant task of explaining. But let us, while disclaiming all responsibility, suppose Ben Jose in possession of all the outward facts of the case, and invited to read their inner meaning by the doubtful light of his suspicions and prejudices. What would he make of it?

Something like this, probably. Steve, a small rogue, attached as jackal to a big rogue—Reseigh—doing all his dirty jobs and risky jobs for him, enjoys in return unlimited credit for brandy, and a measure of contemptuous familiarity and protection. Steve therefore colourably plumes himself on the unenviable distinction of being Reseigh's favourite and confidant, and is weakly proud of his bad pre-eminence. Enter on the scene Paul Carah. Steve, coming into collision with him, and getting the worst of it, conceives for him a violent hatred, which Reseigh sees good to foster. Acting on hints from Reseigh, Steve elaborates and carries out a plan which, he thinks, will have the effect of ruining Paul and driving him out of the place. But Reseigh intends the plan to serve another purpose. For a scheme of his own he needs a sharper, straighter, steadier tool than the thieving, brandy-swilling Steve. Steve delivers his blow; the tool falls into Reseigh's hand, and Steve is straightway discarded. He goes about in comfortable ignorance of this, until Paul's frequent conferences with Reseigh arouse his suspicion. Then he observes Dummy's antics on the pier, and light breaks in upon him. He is supplanted, and by the enemy he thought to have crushed. You know the rest—his rage against Paul and Reseigh finding vent in indiscreet invective, suddenly checked by the appearance of the latter; a stern warning, no doubt, delivered, and Steve reduced to impotent, wrathful brooding over his wrongs.

Sheer melodrama, of course ; for which, as we say, we disclaim all responsibility.

CHAPTER XVIII

HE GROWS UNEASY

A WEEK afterwards, a second expedition was made, equally successful with the first. Then the growing moon put a temporary veto on the proceedings, and Paul, insatiable of excitement, cast about him in search of new fields of activity. The business of fishing, dull and tedious by comparison, had lost its one-time flavour of novelty. He continued to carry it on perforce, but he had sucked all the gay adventure out of it; 'twas a task, a stale routine, of which he was thoroughly sick. He began to dream again of the old days of his continental wanderings, and to contemplate a return to them as a possible contingency.

A temporary diversion was afforded by a new scheme, petty and unimportant, perhaps, in comparison with others of his planning,

Q

but still sufficiently interesting to absorb his thoughts for a while.

It arose like this. Paul came home one evening after a hard day's crabbing, to find Mr Jose poring as usual over his maps. The old man was always prodigal of his ink, and his clumsy fingers were permanently smudged and stained with black. Now Paul had been out after cuttle in the small hours, and consequently his hands were in a worse state of inkiness than Mr Jose's. One cannot handle cuttle without being besmeared and bespattered with the filthy black fluid they carry for their protection. Paul was tired and hungry. He called for his supper, purposing to go to bed immediately afterwards. As he sprawled at the table, eating and yawning, one of his hands happened to rest in close proximity to one of Mr Jose's ; and the latter made a remark about the identical condition of the two. 'Twas just the thing to arrest Paul's attention and excite his imagination. He was wide awake in a moment, instituting an eager comparison. His wits went to work, and before you could say 'knife,' a fully caparisoned scheme sprang Minerva-like from his brain.

Ink! Here was another instance of blind,

senseless wastefulness. Hundreds of cuttle killed weekly in Porthvean, and the most valuable part of them thrown away. Look how his fingers were stained! Rub and scrub as he might, 'twould be days before the marks would be effaced. That'll tell 'ee! What was the essential quality of ink? Permanence, to be sure. Well, then! Could the concoction they sold in shops compare for a moment with this genuine, natural product? Not it; not for goodness, nor for cheapness either. 'Twas the cod-liver oil over again.

Perhaps the closeness of the parallel deterred him; at any rate, for once in a way, he eschewed dazzling possibilities, and kept the new project within moderate and practical bounds. There was no talk of making one's fortune; but Mr Jose need never buy another drop of ink while he lived. Didn't he find that his maps faded after a while? Of course he did, with the mucky, trashy stuff he used. Well, Paul promised him that every map he drew after this should be immortal, carrying its outlines, and his fame with them, glorious and undimmed, to remotest posterity. What did he say? Would he try it?

Mr Jose had his faults, but he never failed

in his whole-hearted belief in Paul's genius. Try it? Of course he would; and by way of graceful compliment to his paragon, the first map he drew should be the United States—the long-contemplated revised edition, with Columbus, Ioway, assigned its true position among great cities. Paul forgot his fatigue, and went off at once to procure the material; and the very next evening, Mr Jose took his seat at the table, a clean sheet of paper before him, a pint jug of cuttle-ink at his elbow, and started without delay on the coast-line of Maine. At his other elbow sat Paul, watching with the deepest interest every stroke of the pen, ejaculating an admonitory 'Steady now!' at the difficult places, and a commendatory 'Well done, auld chap!' when the twisty inlet or what not had been successfully negotiated. When the outline was finished, and Mr Jose began to fill in names of states and cities, Paul's interest was redoubled. The fishing industry suffered severely; every evening he must be on the spot, criticising, suggesting, tracing old itineraries, with a yarn for each mile.

'How the auld days do come back to me!' was a frequent remark, followed by a sigh and 'Those were merry, bustlin' times.'

Then it was—'New Orleans—I never went there. Missed en somehow. Fine place too, so they do tell me. Wish I'd gone.' Then an interval of regretful, vacant - eyed meditation, followed, perhaps, by a panegyrical disquisition on the joys of a wandering life, when a man is his own master—a man, as we say, and no tree, choosing for himself at each cross-road, with no call to hunt for the adventures that throw themselves in his way at every turn.

And at last, one evening, after he had been watching Mr Jose in silence for some time, he began a sentence with seven pregnant words.

'When I go back to the States—' he said.

The pen dropped from Mr Jose's hand.

'What, Paul!' he exclaimed. 'What was that you said? Edn' thinkin' o' goin' away an' leavin' us, are 'ee?'

'S'pose I shall, some time,' he replied indifferently, as one might speak of a trip to Henliston. Then, the notion being broached, he warmed to it, and continued with more animation.

''Course I shall; an' ef 'tes brave an' soon, I shouldn' be surprised. Porthvean edn' a place for a man like me, I can see that. Bistly auld hole! No bustle, no fun, no nothin'. I'm tired o' tryin' to wake 'ee up. You're like Ludlow's dog down here, leanin' agin the wall to bark. Ef I go to stretch my arms here, I belong to knock the walls down. No ; I edn' long for Porthvean, uncle ; make up your mind to that, an' get the dash-an-darras [1] ready.'

Mr Jose tried to rub the shock out of his brain, and left a streak of ink on his forehead. 'What a sudden chap you are! Goin' to leave us ? I dedn' expect—'

The father's eyes rested on Jennifer. One knows of what he was thinking.

'Jennifer, did 'ee hear that ? Paul's thinkin' o' leavin' us !'

Jennifer had heard. When Mr Jose dropped his pen, her fingers had been suddenly arrested (she was knitting), her breathing checked, her whole frame jolted, as it were, with the minute convulsive shock that is caused by a momentary stoppage of the heart's action. But she had not looked up, and instantly she was bending lower over her work, her fingers going with feverish activity.

'Ded 'ee hear, Jennifer ? We'll be brave an' sorry for that, shaan't us ?'

[1] *Dash-an-darras* is the Gaelic *doch-na-dorus*, a stirrup-cup ; literally, 'a cup at the door.'

'Aw ess, s'pose,' she said, and forced an hysterical giggle, which sounded strangely from her lips.

Paul was hurt.

' *You*'ll be sorry, uncle, no doubt,' he said pointedly. ' Arter that, I don't care who's sorry an' who's glad.'

Whether her indifference was feigned or real, she had overdone it. She lifted her eyes.

' I shall be sorry, too, Paul,' she said, quite earnestly—' brave an' sorry.'

Paul grunted, only half appeased.

' Thankful to hear 'ee say so,' he said, and bade Mr Jose go on with his map.

But the incident had the result of fixing in his mind the vague notion he had been entertaining. It took shape as a definite resolution of departure, not just yet, but at some future time, contingent on this and that. One must first see one's way to a dramatic exit. The exciting fun of running contraband still appealed to one. Above all, one needed the sinews of war before embarking on a new campaign.

Now it was a matter for uneasy consideration that the generous Reseigh had suddenly grown close-fisted, not to say stingy. When it came to selling him fish, his offers sank to the market level or below it ; and he haggled and bargained with Paul as keenly as he did with the no-account fellows of the town. Moreover, what was worse, when the bargain was concluded, the cash was not always forthcoming. There were evasions and oblique references to an account standing in Paul's name, very unpleasant to listen to. And as to the contraband profits, he refused altogether to give any account of them, pleading delay in realisation, bemoaning the badness of the times, throwing himself on Paul's mercy, imploring him to wait a little. All very well ; but our confidence, if not overturned, is considerably shaken. The venture brings us fun and excitement, but we look for profit too. Altogether an unsatisfactory state of affairs. We are loth to abandon the high opinion we have formed of the old chap, especially when we remember how loudly we have maintained it in the face of detractors ; but we are grieved and perplexed at this unexpected manifestation of a miserly spirit. We make no scene ; friendship forbids, and not only friendship perhaps, but also the merest suspicion of uneasiness with regard to the big black book and a recent addition to its contents. Not a debt, we know ; we have

Reseigh's assurance for that. But his mind is obviously failing ; he has been positively short with us once or twice of late ; and if he should choose to proclaim it a debt, who could gainsay him ?

About this time, Paul became conscious that he was being watched and spied upon. At first it was merely that vague warning instinct that tells us, independently of our ordinary senses, when the eves of another are upon us. But presently he began to note that wherever he went, afloat or ashore, Steve Polkinhorne was never far away. He did not obtrude himself; on the contrary, he seemed anxious to shun actual meetings ; but there he was, always on the spot, or slinking round it. If Paul went to talk business with Reseigh, when he came out of the parlour he was pretty sure to find Steve in the shop, making pretence to buy a box of matches. If he happened to be chatting with somebody in the street or down by the boats (the *tabu* had been slightly relaxed of late), Steve was sure to sidle up within earshot. When the *Swiftsure* put out to sea, Steve's boat put out too ; and wherever Paul shot his nets, there or thereby Steve did the same.

Other disquieting incidents were conjecturally traced to the same source. A second time the out-house was broken into by night. Nothing was taken, nothing destroyed; but the topsy-turvy condition of the place seemed to indicate that the intruder had entered to search for something which he had failed to find. Again, Paul was ready to swear that his store-pot had been hauled up more than once by unauthorised hands. And once, returning about daybreak from a perfectly innocent crabbing expedition, he fancied he saw the figure of a man sneaking off behind the boats. It was too dark to distinguish who it was. Paul hallooed, and the figure broke into a run and fled. An extremely suspicious circumstance, and one which, when conjoined with the other incidents, gave reasonable cause for considerable alarm. Paul was justified in resolving to keep a sharp look-out, and to smash the face of the first man he caught in the act of prying after him.

CHAPTER XIX

HE IS WARNED

MONDAY night, then!'

'Look 'ee here, Paul; I've tauld 'ee often 'nough not to holler like that when we're talking business. 'A edn' safe.'

'All right, uncle; trust me. 'Tes my way, though, to spake out. A mark o' my natur', 'a b'lieve—open and honest, like-a-thing.'

'That's very well,' grumbled Reseigh, putting the letter with the foreign stamp back into his pocket; 'but 'a edn' safe.'

He waddled to the door and stood arrested with his hand on the latch.

'Could ha' sworn I shut en home,' he muttered. Then suddenly he flung the door open, and looked out into the shop. Paul remained sitting, and heard him address some one in the low distinct tone he affected when annoyed or angry.

' What's doin' here ? ' he asked.

' Jus' buyin' a box o' matches,' came the answer in Steve's voice.

Another voice chimed in—a feminine voice, shrill with irritation.

' Then you med as well buy 'em an' be done, it said. ' Half-an-hour you've been plaguin' an' fussin' round makin' up your mind.'

' You have, have you ? ' It was Reseigh speaking now. ' Well, just you fit and be off. I don't knaw what you're arter, but you'd better look out. I've guv 'ee a talkin' to, wance of late. Sim' me I belong to give 'ee another 'fore long. Get what you want, an' be off.'

A pause, then Steve's voice again, with a curious expression in it.

' I've got what I want, an' I'm off.'

Reseigh came back thoughtful, and sat in a brown study while Paul rehearsed the iniquities of Steve. When he dismissed his musings and sat up, he made a remark *à propos* of nothing.

' Man with a whip,' he said, ' don't pay no 'ttention to a dog that comes sniffin' at his heels. That's so, edn' 'a ? '

Paul agreed. The merest pup knew the

meaning of a whip. But what was Reseigh referring to? Anything to do with Steve?

'Aw no, nothin'. Only a fancy that came into my heed,' said Reseigh. 'But you might keep an eye 'pon the rogue. He dursn't do much harm, but he might give some 'nnoyance f'rall that. He'll be out o' the way 'fore long, 'a b'lieve. An' now you're off, s'pose. Monday night, an' same auld place.'

'Right,' said Paul, and departed.

It was Saturday afternoon, and when Reseigh's summons had disturbed him at his post-prandial pipe, Jennifer was just about to begin her weekly purgatorial task of dusting the parlour. When he returned, he found her sitting in the kitchen; and on the table before her was a dustpan full of shards of broken crockery.

'Hullo!' he exclaimed. 'Been smashin' the cloam?'

'No,' she said.

'How then?' he asked.

'I went in there,' she said, pointing to the parlour door, 'an' found this—'tes wan o' the mugs 'pon the chimney—lyin' broken under the grate. What da'll say, I don't knaw.'

'Say? He'll say you're a careless maid to

liv the door open for the cats to get in. That's what he'll say, an' quite right, too.'

'Paul,' she said, 'you do knaw so well as I that the door's shut home an' locked from Sunday to Sat'day.'

'Pouf! Window, 'course!'

'Window hasn' been open for years. The paint's in the cracks. 'Tes fixed tight.'

Paul began to think, and the more he thought, the more disturbed his face grew.

'Jennifer,' he said, 'I don't like the looks o' this at all. Mug smashed an' nobody done et? An' in that room, too? Jennifer, I've a jealous thought there's somethin' wrong. 'Tes allers a token of evil when cloam do smash; but when et do smash of ets own self—'

His sudden silence was eloquent.

'I don't knaw what da'll say,' Jennifer repeated. The silly girl seemed to attach more importance to that than to the ominous hints and forebodings which were occupying Paul. He waved her trivial worry aside with an impatient hand.

''Tes for wan in the house,' he gloated shiveringly. 'Wan of us three; me, or you, or your da. Sim' me, 'a shouldn' be me, not bein' wan o' the fam'ly. But then They mightn' knaw that. Still, don't see how 'a should be me. You don't think 'tes meant for me, do 'ee, Jennifer?'

'No, Paul,' she said wearily. 'Most like 'tes for me or da, ef 'tes for anybody.'

Somehow he felt accused of selfishness.

'I hope not!' he exclaimed. 'My word fur'n, I hope not. I swear ti' 'ee, Jennifer, I'd rather take et 'pon myself, rather than you or your da should come to harm. But there—'tes fullishness, arter all. Don't 'ee worry, Jennifer; 'tes on'y fullishness. I never set no store by these here tokens. Maybe 'tes for the canary, ha-ha! He's wan o' the fam'ly. Ess, 'tes for he, an' he'll get the pip, sure 'nough, ha-ha! Plum fullishness, edn' 'a?'

His anxiety for support and reassurance was patent.

'Fullishness, 'course,' said Jennifer, assuming light indifference. 'I'm only troubled 'bout da. He'll be brave an' vexed. How's goin' to keep him from knowin'?'

The problem offered a welcome diversion to Paul's thoughts. He pondered and easily found a solution.

'Look! you've got another mug like that somewheres, I'll be bound. Well, then, you fit an' put en in the same place 'pon the chimley. He waan't notice the defference. An' throw the jowds outside, where they waan't be seen. Bistly auld rummage!' he exclaimed, eyeing the fragments with uneasy disfavour.

''Tes cheatin',' said Jennifer, but proceeded to carry out his suggestion without further protest. To give in to Paul, to save her father from annoyance—she asked no more of herself nowadays.

On Sunday afternoon Mr Jose took up the Bible as usual, and went into the parlour. No amount of repetition could rid Paul of the nervous dislike with which he regarded this business of Sunday afternoons; and to-day, after the event of Saturday, he was particularly disturbed. For a while he remained fidgeting about, unable to sit or stand or pace the room for two consecutive minutes; and then, with ''Ere, I caan't stand this. I'm off!' he seized his hat and went out.

When he returned, he found Jennifer still alone, and looking anxious.

'Sim' me, da's a long time to-day,' she said.

'Somethin' up?' said Paul apprehensively.

They said no more, but waited in silence—

a silence that grew more and more oppressive and intolerable as the minutes passed. At last movements were heard in the parlour.

'He's comin' out,' said Paul, with a sigh of relief.

The door opened, and Mr Jose slowly appeared. His face wore an expression of awed solemnity.

'Children,' he said in a slow, breathless voice ; 'Paul, Jennifer, I've had a warnin'.'

He advanced a step or two, blinking like a man who comes from a dark room into the light out of doors.

'I was readin' an' waitin',' he said ; 'an' maybe I'd fallen into a bit of a dose. All of a sudden I woke up, an' there she was. I never seed her so plain before, not sence—well, there she was. An' she was brave an' vexed 'bout somethin', simminly.'

Paul and Jennifer exchanged glances.

'Her heed was shakin',' continued Mr Jose, 'an' her lips were movin' quick—she allers did talk pretty fast—but not a word could I make out. "Spake up, Ellen," said I. An' she opened her mouth an' hollered—but 'twas all the same ; I couldn' hear a word. So I shook my heed, an' her han's dropped down

R

by her side, desp'rate like. So I said, "What's
up, Ellen? Anythin' wrong wi' 'ee?" said I.
An' then she up with her arms an' swayzed 'em
about, slow an' solemn, as ef she was warnin'
me agin somethin'; an' her face was wisht an'
anxious, drawed up with trouble, like. An'
then, 'twas as ef I'd been dreamin' an' waked
up sudden; for all to wance she was gone,
like the snuff of a candle gone out.'

He paused and looked from one to the other.
They were both very pale. Jennifer was
sitting perfectly still; Paul was twitching
about, biting his nails, drumming on the table,
tugging his moustache.

''Tes a warnin', sure 'nough,' he went on;
'a warnin' of evil—evil to this house. The
Lord send us safe through en! Ef we only
knawed—but no: we edn' to be tauld, that's
plain. But there's the warnin'.'

Paul's suppressed terror burst out in the
shape of intense irritation.

'What's the use,' he almost screamed, 'o'
Their comin' to warn us, ef They don't give us
no p'ticulars? That's what I want to knaw:
what's the use? Ef They caan't do no better'n
that, how don't They stay in Their place, an
not come scarin' folk? What's the good of

a warnin' when you don't knaw what you're warned agin?'

'Hush, Paul,' said the old man, much shocked. ''Twas a sort of blasphemy. 'Don't 'ee talk like that. They do Their best, s'pose; an' we belong to be thankful to Them.'

''Tes all nonsense!' shouted Paul, fighting his terror with sounding words. 'I don't believe—'

'Paul!' Mr Jose was actually angry. 'Don't let me hear such talk. 'Tes wicked! Who knaws but They may be listenin'? I edn' goin' to stop an' listen to such talk.'

Deeply offended, he took his hat and trotted out.

Jennifer's face showed great trouble. She hesitated a moment, and then — 'Paul,' she said timidly, 'sim' me you might ask da's pardon presently. He's turr'ble vexed. I never saw him so vexed.'

'Don't care,' said Paul sullenly. 'He shouldn' come plaguin' the life out o' folk with his bistly auld randigals. Fullishness! Sim' me, he must ha' dreamt et all.' He clutched eagerly at the ·heartening notion. 'Ess, course, that's et! Dedn' he say he'd dropped off to sleep? An' dedn' he come out here blinkin'? Ha-ha! the auld chap had too much denner, 'a b'lieve. Ess, 'twas a dream, sure 'nough. Don't 'ee think so, Jennifer? 'Twas a dream, wadn' 'a?'

'Ess, maybe,' said Jennifer. 'An' you'll ask da's pardon?'

'Ef you d' wish. Anythin' to plaise 'ee.' He was good-humoured again. 'No wonder the old chap was upsot. 'A edn' wholesome fur'n to go settin' in there. 'Specially arter a Sunday denner, ha-ha! Fat pork an' tatie cake —there's your token ready-made.'

A pause, and then—'They're wisht things, though, dreams are. They don't mane nothin', but they're wisht things.'

At dusk on Monday evening he left the cottage on his way to the cove. The third ex-pedition was to be made that night. He was embarking on it more to please Reseigh, so he told himself, than for any personal pleasure or profit. He was heartily sick of the whole business. For once in his life he had had a dis-turbed night, with ugly dreams and waking starts. He felt tired and out of spirits, and an indefinite sense of impending evil oppressed him. As he strode along, he was rehearsing his determination, stronger now than ever, of throwing up the game as soon as might be, and returning whence he had come.

Just as he came to the corner where the road turned along the cliff, a small brown creature started from behind a stone, limped across the road in front of him, and disappeared in the hedge.

He stopped dead, shivering like a startled horse.

There could be no mistake; it was a hare, sure enough, and it had run across between him and his purposed trip. Nothing of more terrible omen could have happened. And there was no doubt this time; it was meant for him and nobody else. Steve's abortive blow in the dark was child's play to it. Human agency was responsible for that: but this—! And it was the third on three consecutive days. Ominous number! They were for him; all three were for him. The others were vague, but this one pointed definitely. Evil fortune! It rang in his ears; the growing darkness whispered it, spoke it aloud, shouted it.

One thing was certain. He must abandon all thoughts of going on. He feared no human risk, but this was different. He walked slowly back to the gate. The thought of a small detail arrested his hand on the latch. Reseigh must be informed of the postponement, or the worthy old man would be wondering what was up.

He swung round and retraced his way, not without some qualms on crossing the spot where the hare had passed. He gained the village, went up the street, entered the shop, and—privilege of intimate friendship—passed, without knocking or inquiring, into Reseigh's private room. Reseigh looked up from his accounts. The good old soul was always pottering at his figures; 'twas Ben Jose and his maps over again.

'Well?' he said.

Paul explained. He was sorry to throw the plans into confusion, but there could be no expedition that night.

Oh, indeed! And how was that? Reseigh was curious to know.

There are motives which one does not care to shout from the housetops. In his best off-hand style Paul explained that he didn't feel inclined to go out; he was out of sorts and wanted a comfortable night in bed.

Dear me! Reseigh was brave and sorry to hear that Paul was unwell. But a postponement would mean grave inconvenience and

anxiety. He was afraid he must trouble Paul
to shake off his indisposition and reconsider his
resolve.

Paul flatly refused. He wasn't going out that
night for anybody or anything. Let Reseigh
understand that, and make the best of it.

Reseigh blandly insisted. He had every consideration for his partner's feelings and wishes;
but it was a matter of business, his business
as well as Paul's; and, at whatever inconvenience, business must be done.

Paul grew testy. One would think Reseigh
was a master giving orders to his servant.
They were partners, weren't they? Their
voices carried equal weight. Reseigh said
'Go out.' Paul said 'Stay at home.' As the
action rested with Paul, so naturally did the
decision. And now he was on the subject, he
might tell Reseigh that he was tired of the
whole affair, and he had a good mind to with-
draw from it, unless he saw a better prospect
of profit to himself. Anyhow, he was not going
out that night, as he said, for anybody or anything.

Reseigh, still all honey, pointed out that in
that case, since Paul refused to perform his
part of the contract, the scheme might be said

to have fallen through, and consequently the partnership was to all intents and purposes dissolved.

Paul's temper rose. Very well then. As well now as later on. And, let him tell Reseigh, he was bitterly disappointed in him. He was inconsiderate, he was presuming, and Paul had grave doubts about his honesty. The partnership was dissolved; Paul had said it. Let them settle up and part in friendship while they could.

Just as Paul pleased. And they would settle up at once.

Reseigh got up and went out into the shop, returning immediately with the big black book. He turned over some pages and read out :—

'" To Paul Carah. By gear supplied, February twenty-fourth :—eight pound, four shellin', six pence." Haven't got en in your pocket, s'pose ? '

Paul was dumfounded. ' But—but that edn' a debt ! ' he stammered. ' 'Twas agreed so ; 'a wadn' to be a debt.'

' 'Tes put down for a debt,' said Reseigh suavely, ' so 'a es a debt, s'pose.'

' Edn' nothin' o' the sort ! ' exclaimed Paul,

angry and alarmed. ''Twas for the partnership.'

'What partnership?' asked Reseigh coolly.
'Edn' no partnership, so fur's I knaw. But
there's the gear. Where's the money?'

Paul saw a chance for a firm grip round the
waist. 'Where's *my* money?' he cried trium-
phantly. 'My share in the profits—pay yourself out o' that!'

'Profits? What profits?' Reseigh's face
was a blank.

'Smugglin' profits, thou rogue!'

'Smugglin'? Don't knaw nothin' about
en.'

'Don't knaw! Thou lemb! Don't 'ee try
to putt upon me! I edn' to be putt upon! Pay
me to wance, or I'll—'

'Well?' Reseigh was very grave. 'What
will 'ee do? Smugglin'? 'Tes agin the law,
'a believe? *I* don't meddle wed'n. An' how's
goin' to prove et? I don't pay without no
proofs. Maybe you'd better sue me fur'n up to
county court.'

Paul glared and snapped, a rat in a trap.

'Look, Paul,' said Reseigh, all gentle
suavity, 'I'm allers ready to be'ave honest to
them that be'ave honest to me. You do want to

make out there was a bargain between us.
Well, my mem'ry's a bad wan for some things,
but I'm ready to believe 'ee ef I can believe
you're an honest man. But when an honest
man do make a bargain, he sticks to en.
You do say there's a bargain, an' then you
want to break en. That don't look honest,
do 'a ?'

Paul was utterly bewildered. 'Twas turning
the tables with a vengeance.

'Come,' said Reseigh. 'You called me a
rogue jus' now. 'Tes hard to be called a rogue,
but I forgive 'ee. I don't call *you* a rogue ; I
call you an honest man that sticks to his bargain. An', sim' me, my mem'ry's comin' back
agin. There *was* a bargain ; I mind et now.
An' your part of en was that you should go out
an' do a bit o' business for me to-night. An' I
beg of 'ee, don't say you edn' goin', or my
mem'ry's clane gone for everythin' but what's
down in black an' white in my book.'

His words were gloved in softest velvet, but
their grip was of iron. Paul felt himself held
fast, unable to achieve the merest wriggle. So
this was his meek, submissive ally—this consummate, audacious villain ! 'Twas a hard con-
fession to make, but he had met his match for

once; and the admission was a leak through which all his spirit oozed away.

Reseigh continued. 'Contrariwise, ef you d' go, I'm like to forget what's in the book. Then we're partners agin, an' the debt's no debt. 'A 'll be the biggest haul o' the lot to-night, an' when 'tes safe in my cellar, I'll see what I can do for 'ee. You d' knaw me; I'm easy to deal wi' when I edn' putt upon. When I'm putt upon, I'm hard. Et makes me mis'rable to be hard wi' *you*, Paul; but 'tes my natur'—forgi'e me for that.'

Paul was staring desperately before him. Reseigh stood up and clapped him on the shoulder.

'Come, partner!' he exclaimed, 'where's your sperit? Honest man, where's your honour? Edn' goin' to give in, are 'ee, an' miss all the fun an' profit? 'Tes profit for 'ee this time—my word fur'n; money down, soon's you come back. Edn' afraid o' the risk, are 'ee? Paul Carah afraid!'

He jumped at the sting.

'Afraid, honest partner!' he laughed wildly. 'Not though I stand in the face o' destruction, with an honest partner at my heels! Never say die! There's sperit in me yet. An' while there's sperit in Paul Carah, there's confusion to all rogues. Shake han's, honest partner, an' fare 'ee well. I'm off to say.'

He gripped Reseigh's fingers till they tingled again ; and then, with a rush, he was gone.

CHAPTER XX

HE IS CAUGHT

PAUL rushed down to the quay like one possessed. He dared not allow himself to pause
and reflect, lest the terror at his heels should
overtake him. To stifle thought he must move
and act with desperate energy. If there was a
coherent idea in him, it was that by bustle and
rush he might confuse, as it were, the powers
invisible, and so get away, leaving them baulked
of their spring.

Dummy was waiting by the boat, fretting
and gesticulating about something. As Paul
approached, he ran forward, alternately pointing
to the dark shadows about the fish-cellars, and
making vehement signs, among which one, by
its recurrence, left a faint impress on Paul's
whirling senses. It was the hand to the mouth
and head thrown back, signifying drink to all
the world, and Steve Polkinhorne to Dummy's

familiars. Paul noticed it, and mechanically translated it; and out of his brain it flitted, driven by Dummy himself. Dummy! He had forgotten Dummy. Dummy must not go with him. Strange! in all this welter he realised with extraordinary vividness that he felt a peculiar tenderness for Dummy, his simple, stupid, faithful follower. If Dummy went with him, two would be involved in the fate—whatever it might be—that was meant for one alone. His wits flashed back to him, and at this moment of supreme test, with an unknown horror hanging over him, they worked, as they were apt to work but seldom, for another than himself. Dummy must not go. Dummy must remain safe on shore. It introduced a tangible risk, for the wind was fresh, and the boat was too large for one man to manage with safety; but for that he cared nothing. He must go to meet his fate alone. He must play the game like a man, for it might be the last he would play.

The boat was under the quay, just floating on the rising tide. He strode through the water and swung himself in, waving Dummy back as he prepared to follow. At the gesture Dummy stood, his feet in the water, a picture of blank astonishment. Paul repeated it vehemently. You know the behaviour of a dog who has surreptitiously followed his master out of doors, when he is discovered and ordered home again. Just so behaved Dummy. He turned back a yard or so, faced round, stood staring, advanced a timid step, was waved back, retreated a little farther, stopped again, went forward with desperate assurance, only to be arrested once more by yet another impetuous signal.

Meanwhile Paul was getting the oars out and unfastening the painter. This done, he waved a farewell to Dummy, and pushed off. What was passing in Dummy's mind one cannot tell. Perhaps he read peril in Paul's face, perhaps his dog-like instinct warned him. If peril there was, he could not leave his master to face it alone. As Paul thrust with his oar against the quay wall, Dummy rushed forward, splashed through the water up to his waist, clutched the backward-pointing bow of the boat, and scrambled in. Paul waved a despairing gesture, and resigned himself. He had done what he could. There must be no turning back that night. Fate held the tiller; what was to be must be.

Away from the land, with the fresh sane

wind blowing against his face, and the waves lapping steadily under the bows of the boat, he grew cooler and more collected. He began to regard the situation with a calm, dispassionate interest, as a matter in which he had no personal concern. With some curiosity, with next to no alarm, he wondered what shape his impending fate would assume. He tried to work out a grotesque rule-of-three sum. If one hare's foot was equal to a sprained wrist and an attack of sea-sickness, what result would the whole animal produce ? Then his thoughts wandered altogether away, to the shore he was leaving behind, to the village, to the Joses' cottage. He pictured the scene in the kitchen—the shaded lamp on the table, Ben Jose and Jennifer on either side of it, their faces in a half shadow, their hands moving in a bright light, the father's slowly and steadily guiding his little pen over the paper, the daughter's jerking with swift, short abruptness as they manipulated the gleaming needles. Were they thinking of him ? he wondered. With calm consideration he reviewed the past months, reading them through as he would a story-book. They were interesting, full of vivid incident—he delivered no further judgment on them ; the queer sense of detachment was complete. He felt without hope, without fear, completely purged of all human emotion. 'Twas as if he had broken loose from life already, and sat surveying it from afar.

The appointed spot was reached, exactly at the appointed time. He peered about through the darkness for signs of the approaching vessel. Nothing was to be seen. By agreement, an hour's grace was allowed. The floats of the trammel made blacker spots on the black water hard by. He had not meant to do so, but after all he might as well haul up while he was waiting. It would help to pass the time away. He signed to Dummy, and they set to work.

The trammel was heavy to rending-point with fish. Never since it was first put out had it come up so full. To Paul, it seemed as an ironic joke of Fate, smiling in her grim way on her victim before delivering the blow. He laughed back in her face, not in defiance, but in frank acknowledgment of the humour of the thing.

A light waved up and down in the darkness ahead. Here they were! Paul seized the lantern and swung it thrice in the air. A dim bulk loomed up and swept quickly past. There

S

was an excited chatter of foreign voices, a hail—
' All-a-raight ? '—in broken English, an echoing
response from Paul, the splash of a heavy body
in the water, and the stranger receded, dwindled,
was swallowed up in the night.

They rowed up and hauled in. Three kegs
and two tarpaulined packages were distributed
under the thwarts, the barrel that served as a
buoy was staved in and set adrift, and the boat's
head was turned homewards. Nothing out of
the way had happened so far. As the *Swiftsure*
slipped through the waves, nearer every moment
to home and safety, the brooding horror was
lifted from Paul's spirits, and they rose buoyant.
Nothing had happened yet ; and what could
happen now ? The wind, though fresh,
was fair and steady, his hand was firm on
the tiller, the trusty Dummy was with
him—what was there to fear ? In an hour
he would be stretching his limbs between
the sheets in warm security. Surely the blow,
if it had been delivered, had fallen short, baulked
by his agility, checked by his show of calm
confidence. And was it not all nonsense and
foolishness, as he had ever declared—an old
wives' fable, fit to frighten children, but which it
were shame for a man to heed ?

The land grew up black against the dark sky. Presently the town was to be made out, a grey patch daubed against the cliff, glimmering as if the walls and roofs were giving out a dim phosphorescence stored up in the hours of sunlight. Paul steered in, cautiously watching. The quay was deserted, not a light showed in a window. All was safe; and there was no need for noisy oars; the wind was good to take him right in under the quay.

Quay-head was rounded, the sails came down with a subdued rattle, the boat glided slowly into the shadow of the cliff, and was stayed under the windows of the shop. Paul stood up and gave the signal, a curlew's cry twice repeated. He waited, but nothing stirred. He signalled again, and, after a longer wait, a third time. Still no sign that he was heard. What was up? Had Reseigh fallen asleep while waiting? Paul held anxious debate with himself what to do. Should he go ashore and knock Reseigh up? And knock up half the street too! Or put out again and sink the goods by the store-pot? Scarcely wise, when he suspected that prying hands had been meddling thereabouts. The best plan seemed to be to take his cargo, fish and all, up to the cellars, and leave it there for the present. All this time he was standing, oars in hands, with his face to the bow, keeping the boat steady against the tide with an occasional dip of the blades into the water. Now he leaned forward, pushing a long stroke. In a moment the boat's keel kissed the stones, and he and Dummy leapt ashore and seized the painter.

A round eye of light glared at him suddenly from behind a boat, a clatter of feet and a dropping fire of shouts broke the silence, and half-a-dozen men in blue jackets were round him. His fists went up, he struck one blow, the pebbles clinked as a man fell backwards; and then with a calm—' 'Twas to be,' he dropped his arms and resigned himself.

Two men held him, two were struggling with Dummy, who showed desperate fight, and the other two were ransacking the boat. Dummy was overpowered, though not until a rope was round his wrists; the contraband was thrown ashore and shouldered, and the procession started up the beach.

Paul jerked his captors to a standstill.

' *Would* 'ee mind haulin' up the li'll boat, soase?' he pleaded. ' *She* dedn' knaw what

"A round eye of light glared at him suddenly from behind a boat."

she was about, an' 'a edn' fair she should come to harm.'

The two men behind good-naturedly complied.

'Thank 'ee kindly,' said Paul. 'An' now, forwards.'

On the capstan at the top of the beach a man was sitting, swinging his legs, and singing a traditional stave in a squeaky tenor voice.

> ' A starless night,
> No moon in sight,
> An' no land-waiters handy ;
> Come mates away,
> We're off to say
> To fish for kegs o' brandy.'

It was Steve Polkinhorne, unable to resist the temptation of coming to gloat over his enemy's downfall.

'Haul' tongue, thou lemb!' growled one of the men in disgust, and kicked contemptuously at him in passing.

As they went up the street on their way to the coastguard station, lights twinkled in upper rooms, windows were pushed open, and pale, curious faces were thrust out. At one window there were two faces side by side, and Paul heard a whispered 'Who is 'a?'

''Tes me, Paul Carah, catched smugglin',' he

called out, not in bravado, but simply as one
supplying courteous information. The merest
gleam of elation shone in him when he heard
an amazed, half-admiring murmur of, 'Him
agin? What a chap!' At any rate he had
given Porthvean one more shock of surprise.
Tongues would be clacking to-morrow. If he
never came back, here was an exit dramatic
enough, in all conscience.

CHAPTER XXI

HE IS RESCUED

To Jennifer, sitting listlessly by the fire in the kitchen, her father entered, a newspaper in his hand.

'Jennifer,' he said, ''tes all in the paper 'bout Paul; an' I've brought en round, thinkin' you'd like to hear. Shall I read en out?'

She set her face and nodded.

Mr Jose unfolded the paper, instituted a muttering search, and after scanning three pages in vain, hit on the right place.

'Here 'a es, squeezed in a corner, as ef 'twas nothin' at all,' he said, quite disappointed. 'Now listen. "East Trenwith Petty Sessions. Paul Carah, twenty-eight, an' Albert Edward Hendy, forty-six,"—why!' he broke off, 'that's Dummy, s'pose. His da was Ozias Hendy, sure 'nough; but I never knawed his name before. Wonder how they got hold of en.

Albert Edward—that's our Dummy! Think o'
that—Albert Edward!'

Jennifer's fingers clutched at her gown. 'Go
on, da,' she said, in a close voice.

'Ess, my dear. Where was I? Aw ess—
"Paul Carah, twenty-eight, an' Albert Edward
Hendy, forty-six,"—(Albert Edward!—well,
well!)—"forty-six, were charged with smugglin'
contraband on the night of April 14th, an' also
with assaultin' the preventive officers in the
execution of their duty. On bein' placed in
the dock, the younger prisoner"—(that's Paul,
Jennifer),—"prisoner egzitedly addressed the
bench, assertin' that his companion"—(that's
Dummy),—"was deef an' dumb, and totally
incapable of understandin' the natur' of his
offence or of the charge brought against him.
To a question from the magistrates the officer
in charge replied, cor-robbyratin' the statement,
an' addin' that the man was a well-known
char'cter in the district,"—(that's right! they've
got en right; everybody do knaw Dummy, sure
'nough,)—"district, an' was little more than a
harmless idiot." (Idiot! That's so much as
they d' knaw about et!) "On hearin' this,
the Bench ordered the prisoner Hendy to be

released, sayin' that he should never have been brought before them."'

Mr Jose laid the paper down, beaming.

'Dummy's all right then,' said he. 'They hadn' the heart to do nothin' to he. An' Paul stood up fur'n. Magistrates or no magistrates, he wouldn' stand by an' see harm come to Dummy. He spoke up to wance, like the brave chap he allers was. Noble, wadn' 'a, Jennifer? Not a word for hisself; 'twas on'y Dummy he guv a thought for. Noble, wadn' 'a?'

She did not voice her assent. 'Go on, da,' she said.

Mr Jose took the paper up again. '"The charges against Carah were then gone into. Evidence was given of the smugglin' an' of the assault, an', the prisoner offerin' no defence, the magistrates imposed fines amountin' altogether to fifty pounds, or in default, three months' imprisonment?" Fifty pound! Three months! 'A 'll be Bodmin fur'n, I'm afraid. How's goin' to pay all that? · Fifty pound!' He glanced again at the paper. 'Hullo! Here's another bit. "Some egzitement was caused in court by the be'aviour o' the man Hendy, who, when the prisoner was removed, attempted to follow him. It was necessary to use force to prevent it. The uproar he raised at this was so great that the magistrates ordered him to be ejected." Poor chap! He knawed there was somethin' wrong, an' he belonged to stand by his friend. Poor chap! what 'a 'll do without Paul I don't knaw. An' we shall miss him too, sim' me. Brave an' queeat we shall be, without the bustlin' ways of en, an' the loud spache of en. Kep' us goin', he ded, sure 'nough.'

The paper dropped from his hands as he mused.

'Nothin' but things happenin' ever sence he came here. Seven years away, and six months here; put the wan agin the other, an' there's more happened in the six months. "*I*'ll wake 'em up," said he to me wance; an' so 'a ded, sure 'nough. Never was such a wan for bustlin' and schemin'; an' yet, somehow—' he hesitated in a puzzled way—'somehow, nothin' do seem to come of et all. They're talkin' a lot 'bout en over to cove, an' I said to Jim Boase, said I—"Give en a better chanst than he's had, an' he'd 'a been a rich man 'fore now." An' Jim, he said to me, "Ben," said he, " et's well a wild cow has short horns, or creation 'ud be upsot brave an' quick." That's what Jim said to me, manin' the sayin' for Paul. Poor chap! A pretty place all his schemin' 's landed him in.'

He woke from his musings to find Jennifer kneeling beside him, her eyes shining.

'Daddy dear,' she said in a low eager tone, 'we do belong to get him out.'

'We, my dear! How?'

'Look! There's the money you've saved—two hundred pound, edn' 'a? An' 'tes for me, edn' 'a? Fifty pound out o' that do leave a brae lot yet—more than I look to have. How shouldn' we send en to Paul, to get him out?'

'Jennifer! The money I've scraped an' saved for 'ee, so's you should be comfortable, when I edn' here no longer!'

'Don't matter 'bout me,' she urged. 'I can work. Don't matter, so's we can save Paul from disgrace. Paul in prison! 'Twill kill him. Send en off to wance, daddy, I beg of 'ee!'

Mr Jose pondered, eagerly watched.

'No!' he said firmly. 'Et can't be done. I'm brave an' fond o' Paul, an' I'm brave an' sorry fur'n, an' I do wish to help en—but fifty pound o' your money, no! Mus' think for you first, li'll maid. You're my cheeld; Paul edn'. You're a weak woman; Paul's a man, an' do

belong to stand on his own feet. Fifty pound!
No, no, et caan't be done.'

'Daddy, I beg of 'ee!' The tears were in her
eyes. 'Haven't 'ee always said Paul was wan of
us—wan o' the fam'ly?'

Mr Jose shook his head. 'That's on'y in a
manner speakin',' he said, 'jokin', like. 'Sides, I
thought—' he broke off, glancing at her, and a
cunning expression came into his face. 'Wan o'
the family! Now ef there was any chanst o'
that; ef you an' he—'

'Don't, daddy!'

'Listen to me, Jennifer. Ef there was anythin' between 'ee, now, 'twould be defferent.
Then what's yours 'ud be his. I've never spoke
ti' 'ee about et, but you d' knaw how I wish en
to be. Ef you can tell me 'tes like to be as I
do hope fur'n to be, I'll g' up wi' the money to-
morrow, so I will. Come, li'll maid o' mine, tell
your auld da. Has Paul ever said anythin'
ti' 'ee?'

For a moment she was ready to forswear herself, and save Paul with a yes. But she saw the
uselessness of it and the danger of it. Her head
dropped, and—'nothin',' she said.

'Nor he edn' like to?'

'No.'

Mr Jose sighed. ' I, do believe, ef you'd trated en defferent, he'd ha' spoke,' he said, with a spice of reproach. 'I'm sure he's fond of 'ee, or ready to be so. An' you couldn' find a smarter chap nowheres. But you allers were a strange maid. I love 'ee, dear, I'm proud of 'ee ; but—well, 'tes your natur'. I don't say nothin' agin natur'. I do believe what you say, an' I caan't help feelin' sorry fur'n. An' I'm sorry for Paul ; but since 'tes as you say, he mus' look out for his own self.'

She knew on what an inflexible foundation his easy-going nature was built. She could tell by his voice and manner when the foundation was reached. There was no help for Paul from this quarter. Whence, then ? She thought and thought—that which was within her lending her with a supreme clarity to see, a supreme steadiness to weigh and judge. She thought and thought, and a hope came to her, and a determination. A desperate hope, and a desperate venture, but desperate courage was there to urge her on.

She waited till night closed in. Then she put a shawl over her head and went across to the village. At the shop-door she stopped and entered. The girl behind the counter stared at her. Jennifer in the village was a rare sight; Jennifer in Reseigh's shop was almost unique. Porthvean knew next to nothing about her; there were no fetters on its imagination; to what its imagination evolved it cheerfully committed itself; so the girl stared.

Jennifer asked to see Reseigh. He was in the parlour, the girl said, but she would call him.

No; Jennifer wished to see him alone; she would go in to him. Her heart fluttered as she walked across to the door; but her head was clear and cool, and the hand she laid on the latch was quite steady.

Reseigh was sitting in a comfortable arm-chair, his fat hands folded before him, enjoying the good man's well-earned rest after labour. He objected, as the best of men will, to being disturbed after business hours; and when the door opened, he called out quite crossly, telling the intruder to be off and not come plaguing him. Then he looked up and saw Jennifer. His features had learned to repress all involuntary movements in the iron school of his will; but for a moment they forgot themselves, and allowed his surprise to show itself. Then in a flash they were a blank mask. He knew little of Jennifer, but he knew enough to judge that no trivial errand had brought her to his shop, and, unbidden, into his presence.

'Well, my dear, what can I do for 'ee?' he said affably. He was always polite when he saw no reason to be otherwise.

'I've come to spake ti' 'ee,' said Jennifer.

'Ess, well? Set 'ee down. What is 'a?'

'I'll stand,' said Jennifer. ''Tes about Paul I've come.'

'Have 'ee now? An' what about en, I wonder.'

'Paul's in prison,' she said.

'So 'a es, the fullish fellow. I'm sorry fur'n, but he's a fullish fellow.'

'Paul's in prison,' she continued steadily, 'an' 'tes all through you that he's there.'

If he had been walking on the quay, and one of a heap of fish had suddenly reared itself up and denounced him as an infamous trafficker in the flesh of its brethren, he could not have been more genuinely astonished. He was actually impelled to laugh.

'What nonsense are 'ee a-tellin' of, my dear?' he said genially. 'All through me? Sim' me, you edn' azackly. You'd better fit an' go home.'

'All through you,' she repeated. 'You spoke
en fair, an' led en on, an' put this business into
his head, that he'd never ha' thought upon else.
You made en think he was doin' a fine thing.
He never saw nothin' but good in you; he
always stood up for you. An' you've brought en
to ruin. 'Twas for you he went out; you sent
en. An' now he's in Bodmin, an' the fault's
yours.'

Reseigh was more amused than ever. 'There's
a pretty li'll ballat for 'ee!' he said in good-
humoured contempt. 'An' not a word o' truth
in et from beginnin' to eend. An' supposin'
there was—jus' supposin' for the sake of argy-
ment—what then?'

'I look for 'ee to get him out,' said Jennifer.

'Oho!' he exclaimed softly. 'That's et, is 'a?
I'm to pay fifty pound to get a rogue out o' jail,
am I? Out o' friendship, like? Fif-ty pound!'
The sum seemed to swell immeasurably on his
lips. 'Beggin's your arrand, then? An' for fifty
pound!'

'I don't beg o' *you*,' she said. 'I do knaw
better'n that. Edn' beggary to ask a right; an'
that's what I'm doin'. 'Twas through you he
was catched; 'tes for you to get en out.'

The good man was unused to such language.

He may be pardoned for losing his temper a little.

' Aw! 'tes for me to get en out, is 'a?' In his irritation he abandoned his pretended ignorance. 'The rogue's lost me a matter o' ten pound already through his carelessness. An' now I'm to throw fifty more into the say, am I? Sorry for 'ee, my dear, but without you do pay the fine yourself, he mus' rot in jail, mus' your fancy man.'

She never flinched at the insult. 'You've got to get en out,' she repeated. 'An 'a 'll be the worse for 'ee ef you don't.'

A threat! 'Off wi' 'ee,' he said roughly. 'Out o' this house to wance! I've no time to listen to such stuff. An' let me tell 'ee they that do threaten me are like to be sorry fur'n arterwards. Off you go!'

' Ef I go,' she said, ' I go up to the coastguard cap'n, to tell en there's smuggled goods in your cellar.'

She spoke quietly, but she trembled. All depended on the shape Reseigh's caution had taken, whether he had removed the goods and disposed of them at once, or whether he had judged it safer to keep them by him for a while. The sight of his face set her fears at rest, and

T

her heart a-leaping. For a moment he sat
paralysed; then for once in his life the mask
fell completely away, and he burst forth in a
torrent of evil speech. She waited till he
checked himself abruptly, and fell into a sullen
meditation. After a minute's silence, she moved
towards the door.

'Wait!' he said sulkily. She paused, while
he continued to reflect. Presently he looked up
with cunning eyes.

'Ef they're there,' he said,—'I don't say
they are—but *ef* they are, who's to tell they're
smuggled?'

''Tes for you to show they're not,' she said.
'Sim' me, they'll ask you to show the receipts.'

'That's so, sure 'nough,' he said, and thought
again. Again he looked up, and now his face
showed what was meant for frank admiration.

'You're a sharp wan!' he exclaimed heartily.
'For a queeat li'll maid, you're a sharp wan.
The auld chap's fairly beaten. Ess, you've got
the better o' me this time, an' there edn' many
can say that. I don't bear no malice. My
life! what a sharp wan you are!'

If he thought to disarm her with flattery, he
failed. 'The money,' she said.

'Ess, 'tes all right. I'll send en to him. I'll send en to-morrow, never you fear.'

'No,' she said. 'You'll give en to me now.'

'Dost doubt my word?' cried injured innocence. 'I pass my word I'll send en to-morrow. What more do 'ee want?'

'I want the money,' she said. 'There wouldn' be no 'ccasion for 'ee to send en to-morrow. The goods 'll be gone 'fore then. Gie me the money.'

'D'ye suppose,' he snarled, 'I keep all that money by me? Fifty pound! Ef I've got so much in all the world, I'm richer than I thought for. I caan't give what I haven' got, can I?'

'You're a savin' man,' she said; 'you've got en. You're a careful man; you've got en by 'ee. Gie me the money.'

The reiterated demand was like a blank wall, against which he ran his head at every evasive twist.

'No!' he ejaculated, and swore as profusely as if the metaphor was a statement of fact. Without another word, she turned away to go. He threw up his hand.

'Stop! you shall have en,' he growled. In silence he went to his desk and unlocked it. A pile of notes rustled between his fingers; she wondered if he could hear her heart beat above the rustle. The little sounds of movement were portentously magnified in her ears—his heavy breathing, the flutter of papers, the chirping of the keys in his hand, the thud of wood on wood as he closed the desk, the metallic click when he turned the lock, and behind all, the indifferent, inconscient murmur of the sea without.

He turned about, and 'twas as if all the evil passions in this world had flown together and settled on his face. Jennifer's eyes were on his hand and the bunch of notes in it. She stretched out her hand.

'Hauld on!' he said in a voice of venom. 'How am I to knaw where this money's goin' to? 'Tes a brae lot, a temptin' lot. Maybe Paul 'ull have to stop in jail arter all.'

She looked at him, and stretched forth her hand again.

'An' ef you do send et, you'll get the credit, 'course, 'stead o' me.' It was certainly hard, when one was performing a good action, even if against one's will, to think that another was in a position to appropriate the glory of it.

'Shall be in your name,' she said coldly. 'He'll never knaw I had a hand in et.'

'So you say,' he sneered.

' So I say,' she replied. ' Gie me the money.'

He flung the notes on the table. She gathered them up, and turned to go. As she went out into the shop, he followed her. Two women were at the counter, being served. In their presence, and for their benefit, he dealt a parting stab in her back.

' You're well matched, you an' your man. Jail-bird an' light woman—you're a pair.'

Her remaining strength took her safely through the street and past the last of the straggling houses along the cliff. Then the tension snapped. She stumbled off the road and sank on the hedge-bordering grass, shivering and sobbing, utterly wearied and supremely happy.

CHAPTER XXII

HE DEPARTS

IN the kitchen Mr Jose was making feeble attempts to smoke an after-dinner pipe. Jennifer was quietly cleaning away the dishes, and Dummy was sitting in a corner, his elbows on his knees, his chin on his hands, his face contracted with puzzled anxiety. The canary was singing its loudest and merriest, and as Jennifer went out to the door with a basin of dish-water, she stopped and chirruped to it. Mr Jose made a gesture of irritation.

'Sim' me, Jennifer,' he said, 'you edn' got much feelin' in 'ee. How can you be so cheerful? Even Dummy, poor chap, do take on more'n you do. Look at en—there he goes agin!'

For the hundredth time in the past few days Dummy jumped up, clutched at Jennifer's arm, and imitated Paul's characteristic gait, with a

gesture of vehement inquiry to follow. And
for the hundredth time Jennifer assured him, as
plainly as hands and face could speak, that Paul
was coming back to-morrow.

'Poor Dummy,' mused the old man. 'A brae
many to-morrows before you see your partner
agin. My heavens! I knawed I should miss
en, but I never thought to miss en so much.
Every minute I look to hear en come stavin'
along, whistlin' an' singin'? In he comes,
"Hullo, uncle?" says he, an' bangs down 'pon a
chair, fit to smash the legs of en. "Where's
denner?" says he. "Hurry up wi' my denner,"
says he. He allers was a rare wan for his
vittles. But there!—there wadn' nothin' but
what he took an int'rest in. Sim' me, that's
what made him such good comp'ny. This here
life's a dull business to most, but wi' he 'twas as
ef he was diggin' your ribs all the while, p'intin'
out the int'rest of en—fun in this, roguery in
that. An' now he's gone, 'tes as ef the taste o'
life's gone too. Aw me! I do feel kind o'
tired.'

Jennifer lifted her hand, listening.

'Here 'a do come,' she said in a low, glad
voice.

The old man started. 'Who? Paul? My

nerves! you made me jump. You shouldn', my
dear; you shouldn' play tricks like that. Edn'
no fun in be'avin' so.'

'Tes he, daddy; I edn' jokin'. Do 'ee think
I don't knaw his step?'

'Paul? How can 'a be?' But he listened
and heard a step crunching on the path, a quick,
impetuous, familiar step. Then through the
window a momentary glimpse of swinging arms
and stooping head, and as they sprang to their
feet, Paul stood among them, grasping hands all
round, laughing, shouting, as of old.

'Hullo, uncle! Dummy, auld chap! Jennifer!
Dedn' expec' to see me, ded 'ee? Guv 'ee all
a surprise, aha! That's my way. I'm glad
to be'old 'ee all agin. Looks to me as ef you
were glad too. Heya, Dummy! Look at the
chap! He'll have a fit direckly. Had denner,
I see. Fit an' get me a crust, will 'ee, Jennifer?
I'm rawnish.'

Mr Jose slapped his thigh delightedly. 'The
same auld Paul!' he laughed. 'Just the same!
Edn' changed a bit. Glad to be'old 'ee, sonny?
I should think so! But, how came you to come
back so soon?'

'Uncle,' said Paul impressively, 'never you

say another word agin Reseigh so long as you
live.'

'How?' exclaimed Mr Jose. 'Dost mane
to say—?'

''Twas he that got me out; that's what I d'
mane to say.'

'Reseigh?'

'Reseigh an' no mistake. I asked about et
arterwards. The money was sent in a letter, an'
I see the letter. 'A wadn' in Reseigh's fist, but
there was his name, sure 'nough. There's a
friend for 'ee! I went over to thank en, 'fore
come here, but the maid said he was out. But
there's a true friend for 'ee! An' to think that
last time I see him I was angry wed'n, an'
profaned agin him, the good auld man! But
never you say a word more agin him!'

'I waan't,' said Mr Jose humbly. 'I couldn',
arter that. But I'm puzzled, to tell 'ee the
truth. 'A edn' like Reseigh to pay away fifty
pound without he's fo'ced to.'

'There you go agin!' cried Paul irritably.
'There wadn' nobody fo'ced him. He's an
hon'rabble man. I stood by en, I never spoke
his name; I went to prison fur'n, you may say.
'Course, he feelt bound to stand by me an' help
me out. A good, hon'rabble man, I tell 'ee, an'

a true friend as ever was. Now that I'm
leavin' the auld place agin, there edn' many I'm
sorry to say good-bye to, but Reseigh's wan of
'em.'

'Paul! you're talkin' o' leavin' already, an'
you not back home five minutes. But you edn'
goin' jus' yet, s'pose?'

'Soon's I've finished the crust Jennifer's
gettin' for me.'

Clumsy Jennifer let fall the plate she was
carrying. The clatter started Mr Jose's eyes
from Paul's face, but in a moment they were
back again, staring in a stound.

'Paul!'

'Ess, uncle, I'm off this time for sure. All
this while I've been makin' my plans, an' now
'tes settled. Back to the States I go. I edn' for
Porthvean no longer.'

'Paul! you'll wait a bit 'fore go. You'll liv
us see you for a bit, an' get used to the notion.
You allers were a sudden chap, but you'll wait a
bit wi' your friends, won't you?'

'Not I, uncle. I'm sorry to leave 'ee, but I
edn' wan to wait. When I'm set upon a thing,
I go fur'n to wance—that's me! No diddlin'
about for Paul Carah. Haelf an hour, an' I'm

off. Nothin' to keep me here, 'a b'lieve—not even a swettard, aha, Jennifer?'

She was in his confidence; she knew his views on that subject; and he gaily winked at her as she set a plate before him. He fell to with a zest. Mr Jose watched him with a melancholy interest, prattling his regrets the while.

''Twas to be, uncle,' said Paul, as he pushed his plate away. 'I belonged to go back as I came. 'Fore ever I set foot in the place, I had a warnin' how 'a was to be. I never tauld 'ee 'bout that, did I? Strange 'a was, sure 'nough.'

He related the story of the flock of plovers and the solitary bird. 'An' now the token's come true,' he concluded in a suitable tone of dramatic melancholy. 'Off I go into the dark, alone, like the bird.'

'Not alone, Paul!' cried Jennifer, her heart bursting into speech at last. 'Not alone; our good wishes do go with you.'

' Ess, that's so, Paul,' her father added earnestly. ' Jennifer do say right; our best wishes 'll follow 'ee wherever you d' go.'

Paul was touched. 'Then they mus' look to v'yage a brae long way,' he laughed, ashamed to show it. Then he was ashamed of his laughter. 'But 'tes good of 'ee to say so, an' I thank 'ee both fur'n. 'Tes good to think I do leave friends behind. But, bless you, they d' knaw me out in the States. I've fifty friends there for wan over here. That's the place for me. Hooraw for the States ! I'll go an' put up my things to wance.'

Up the stairs he clattered, and the silent folk below could hear him whistling and singing as he stamped about over their heads. In five minutes he was down again, bundle in hand.

'All my worldly goods !' he exclaimed, flourishing it ; 'barrin' a knife an' five shellin's in my pocket.'

'Paul,' said Mr Jose eagerly ; 'ef I can—'

'Stop there, uncle !' he interrupted. 'I d' knaw what you're agoin' to say, but you mus'n' say et. I don't want nothin' but my fingers an' my brain to get along wi'. I shall do very well, never you fear. Gum !' he broke off, 'look at Dummy ; he caan't make out what's up.'

Dummy's attention had been arrested and his imagination excited by the bundle. He was hovering about it, examining it dubiously, and casting uneasy glances at Paul. A bundle meant a journey. It was Paul's bundle. Was his newly-restored friend and master about to desert him again already ?

'Poor Dummy !' Paul exclaimed pityingly.

' Ess, auld chap, I'm goin' to leave 'ee agin, an'
'tes for good this time. You'll have to fit an'
find another partner. My ivers!' he cried,
suddenly deserting pathos for animated narrative. 'That minds me o' somethin' I clane
forgot to tell 'ee. When I come out o' the
station at Henliston this mornin', I see the back
of a man in front o' me. Thinks I, I knaw that
man. So I staved along an' catched him up;
An' who d'ye think 'a was? 'Twas Will Oliver,
the man that sold me the boat. An' such a
wisht, wretched-lookin' chap as he was, I never
see. "Hullo, soase!" said I. "You mind me?'
So he stared at me, mis'rable like, an'—"Ess,
I mind 'ee," he said slowly. "Where you from?"
said he. "Bodmin Jail," said I, for I edn'
ashamed to liv 'em knaw. "Where *you* from?"
said I. "London," said he, "an' a worse place
than jail." "How?" said I. "Hell!" said he, an'
'a made me jump, the way 'a said et. "Curse the
men that built et!" garmed he. "Curse the
ground et's built on! I'm out of en at last,"
said he, "but I've left my money behind, an' my
stren'th, an' my hope. An' I'm goin' home to
my wife an' a cheeld I never set eyes on, an'
we're all goin' to starve together,' says he. An'
then, ef 'a dedn' start snoolin' like a baby, call

me a Devon man to wance! So a thought
come to me, an', said I, "Cheer up, soase," said I.
"Look," said I, "you sold me your boat." "I d'
knaw that," said he, bitter like. "Well," said I,
"ef you've a mind to take en back, you can do so.
I've guv up fishin'," said I. So he laffed, an' 'a
wadn' pretty to hear en. "I'm in rags, as you
d' see," said he, "an' there's holes in my pockets.
All the money's kind o' slipped out," said he.
So I said, "Money I don't want." "How?" said
he. "Thanks is all I do want," said I. "Take
the li'll boat, you're welcome," said I. That's
what I said to en, for et come into my mind
that I had bested en to g'up to London, an' no
man shall put the fault of his ruin 'pon me. So
"Take the li'll boat," said I ; an' you should ha'
seen the face of en. Thanks! Ef thanks were
gold, I'd have a sackful, sure. Ess, I guv the
li'll boat away as ef 'twas nobbut a pair of auld
boots. An' I don't take no credit fur'n nuther."

All the same, he beamed round for applause.
Just like Paul, thought the one who knew him
best ; — as careless and uncalculating in his
generosity as in his selfishness, and as deter-
mined as ever to give his right hand the fullest
information of the doings of his left hand.

'But come!' he exclaimed, starting up,

'mustn' stay yarnin' here. I'm off. Come to
the gate, all of 'ee, an' see the last o' Paul
Carah.'

As he strode out, the garden lay before him,
patched all over with bright green. He paused,
and an expression of genuine emotion now first
appeared on his face.

'Lookin' grand, edn' 'a?' he said. 'There's a
brave scheme all come to nothin'. Ef I wadn'
goin' away, I'd—I've a mind to—Pouf! What
am I a-tellin' of? There's other plans, an'
bigger wans, in my heed now. Forward,
Paul!'

He hurried to the gate, and turned to await
them.

'An' now, good-bye, friends all. Good-bye,
li'll house. Good-bye, uncle; stick to your
maps. Good-bye, Dummy; good-bye, Jennifer.
I'll send 'ee all a letter 'fore long, an' you mus'
write back. An', ha-ha!—look, Jennifer! Ef
Dummy's got his four-master by then, you
mus' liv me knaw, an' I'll send 'ee a tay pot for
a weddin' present.'

Dummy, realising the situation completely at
last, was blubbering profusely. Mr Jose blinked
and blew his nose. Jennifer's eyes were dry,

unnaturally dilated, fixed on Paul with an unwinking stare.

Paul lingered, seeking a final dramatic word. But it would not come. Somehow, at the last moment, with his hand on the gate, a true and deep emotion mastered him. Dear, kindly folk —'twas a wrench to part with them. He never thought to feel it so much. The name of friend suddenly had a new meaning to him; he realised that tendrils from without had, all unknown, penetrated his self-contained, self-enclosed nature. In the presence of the great commonplaces of life — birth, death, meeting, parting—all but the most commonplace words are apt to fail us. And so Paul found it.

'Friends, good-bye,' he repeated over and over again. 'Good-bye, friends. My heart's sore to leave 'ee. Ess, there's grief in my heart to leave 'ee, friends. True friends, we won't forget wan another. Maybe I'll come back some day; ess, sure, I'll come back to my friends.'

He stood dumb for a moment; and then, with one more abrupt, almost savage, 'Good-bye, friends,' he turned and hurried away.

Up the hill, at the turn of the road, he looked back to wave his hand. The three figures were like statues at the gate. Once more the new-found word came to his lips.

'Friends! I'm leavin' true friends behind me.'

Yes, and one who was something more, if he only knew.

THE END

London : 10 Henrietta Street
Covent Garden, W.C.

A Selected List

of

Books

published by

Mr James Bowden

Telegraphic Address :
" Reperuse, London "

TWELFTH THOUSAND.

Joseph Hocking's Great Romance.

Crown 8vo, cloth gilt, 3s. 6d.

The Birthright

By Joseph Hocking,

Author of "All Men are Liars," "Andrew Fairfax," &c.

With Illustrations by Harold Piffard.

OPINIONS OF THE PRESS.

"This volume proves beyond all doubt that Mr Hocking has mastered the art of the historical romancist. 'The Birthright' is, in its way, quite as well constructed, as well written, and as full of incident as any story that has come from the pen of Mr Conan Doyle or Mr Stanley Weyman."—*The Spectator.*

"We read Mr Hocking's book at a sitting; not because we had any leisure for the task, but simply because the book compelled us. . . We hold our breath as each chapter draws to an end, yet cannot stop there, for the race is unflagging. . . . We congratulate Mr Hocking upon his book, for it is a great advance upon anything he has done. We prophesy a big public for 'The Birthright.'"—*The Daily Chronicle.*

"'The Birthright' will be appreciated on account of its successions of exciting scenes, its crisp dialogue, its play of varied character, and a certain eerie air of superstition with which it is pervaded. . . ."
—*The Daily Mail.*

"A thoroughly enjoyable romance. . . . Mr Hocking has woven a story which few will lay down unfinished. The interest never flags for a moment, and the faithfulness with which the scenery of the land of Tre, Pol and Pen is described, and the quaint dialect and traditions of its older inhabitants are reproduced, is beyond praise."—*Weekly Times.*

"We feel certain that, were we still condemned to go to bed at nine, we should sleep with the book under our pillow, and wake with the birds to see what happened. . . . A capital story of its class."—*The Star.*

London: 10 *Henrietta Street, Covent Garden, W.C.*

EIGHTH THOUSAND.

UNIFORM WITH 'THE BIRTHRIGHT.'

Crown 8vo, cloth gilt, 3s. 6d.

And Shall Trelawney Die?

By Joseph Hocking,

Author of " The Birthright," " All Men are Liars," etc.

With Illustrations by Lancelot Speed.

OPINIONS OF THE PRESS.

" 'There is nothing pessimistic nor *fin de siecle* in Mr Joseph Hocking's writings, but a bright, hopeful tone; an air, as we may say, of goodness; genuine romance in treating love, with real feeling for all the ties of home life. Last year he wrote a good Cornish tale, and this year's book ' And shall Trelawney Die? ' is, perhaps, even better."—*The Guardian.*

" The two Cornish tales contained in Mr Hocking's new book are admirable stories, quite simple in construction, related in vigorous English, replete with exciting scenes, and abundantly enriched with local colour. It were but the barest justice to the novelist to admit that they held our attention in tight grip from start to finish."—*The Echo.*

" For thrilling interest and local colouring they are worthy of a place besides ' Q's ' well-known stories. . . Two of the best stories of the year."—*Methodist Times.*

"Interesting and well told, and enriched by the local colour and knowledge of the characteristics of Cornish men and women which distinguish Mr Hocking's books."—*St James's Gazette.*

"An engaging and fascinating romance. . . . The reader puts the story down with a sigh, and wishes there were more of these breezy Cornish uplands, for Mr Joseph Hocking's easy style of narrative does not soon tire."—*Weekly Sun.*

"Vigorous and healthy. Mr Hocking has a fine appreciation of the inner significance of wild Cornish scenery, while his consistent devotion to one corner of England gives him an intimate knowledge and mastery of detail that are extremely valuable."—*The Star.*

London : 10 *Henrietta Street, Covent Garden, W.C.*

THIRD EDITION.

Crown 8vo, cloth gilt, gilt top.   Price 6s.

Methodist Idylls

By Harry Lindsay.

OPINIONS OF THE PRESS.

" A book which in its lovely prose chapters gives an insight into the true romance, the April sunshine, of Methodist life. Mr Harry Lindsay has won our gratitude for the string of stories truthfully entitled ' Methodist Idylls ' which he has just given to the world. . . . We hope that the volume may find its way into every Methodist home. . . . It is, we conceive, in the very highest degree a useful book."—*Methodist Recorder.*

" Never has the life that is lived among our people been handled more tenderly than in ' Methodist Idylls ' by Harry Lindsay. . . . A very helpful and right religious book. . . . The reading of it has been a real joy to us."—*Methodist Times.*

" Mr Harry Lindsay's book ' Methodist Idylls ' is a most admirable attempt to throw into permanent form some portraits of the old and vanishing methodist.   Nothing finer than Simeon Qandy have I ever met with as the portrait of a good, old-fashioned, genuine ' local,' and the other characters are all so true to life that of at least one or two of them I imagined I had known the originals, although I have never been in Gloucestershire in my life."—*The Sun.*

" Harry Lindsay's volume of ' Methodist Idylls ' belongs to the most enduring order of fiction.   These unadorned annals of simple life will suit every season and all moods.   They are for Sunday as well as Saturday, and, however much fashions in fiction may change, they will be found to possess a permanent interest and beauty. . . . They deal with the tenderest and holiest emotions of life, and the supreme points of human experience."—*Dundee Advertiser.*

" Simeon, the outspoken, tender-hearted old peasant preacher, is a splendid character."—*Pall Mall Gazette.*

" These ' Methodist Idylls ' arrested our attention on the first page and held us enthralled to the last, by the sheer force of their consummate skill and deep human interest. . . . In the new fiction which the season has produced we have met nothing so convincing, so thoroughly unaffected, and so faithful to life as the stories which go to make up this book."—*The Independent and Nonconformist.*

London : 10 *Henrietta Street, Covent Garden, W.C*

A UNIQUE AND SPLENDID GIFT BOOK.

Large Crown 8vo, handsomely bound, cloth gilt, gilt top, 6s.

Pictures from
The Life of Nelson

By W. Clark Russell.

With a Photogravure from the famous "Hoppner" portrait, by special permission of H.M. The Queen, and eight full-page illustrations.

The Daily Mail says—"Mr Clark Russell catches the attention of the careless with this series of scenes from the hero's story—scenes glowing and vigorous, and so highly coloured with personal matter as to have all the vivid interest of a novel."

The Review of Reviews says—"A handsome gift book for any boy who is interested in the sea. . . . Full of life and colour; fascinating reading."

Lord CHARLES BERESFORD says—"I think it a splendid boys' book. The advantage of placing Nelson's life and work before the great mass of his countrymen (to whom standard works have been forbidden ground on account of their price) cannot be over-rated."

SECOND AND REVISED EDITION.

Crown 8vo, cloth gilt, gilt top, 2s. 6d.

Victorian Literature

Sixty Years of Books and Bookmen
By Clement K. Shorter,

Author of "Charlotte Brontë and her Circle," &c.

The Times says—"The cleverest retrospect of the literature of the reign that we have seen."

Truth says—"Mr Shorter's 'Victorian Literature' is a model of the art of putting the greatest number of things in the least possible space, in the neatest possible way, and in the handiest possible manner. It will take a permanent place as the most clear, succinct, well-written, and judicial of handbooks of literary reference."

London: 10 *Henrietta Street, Covent Garden, W.C.*

STORIES OF LOWER LONDON.

Crown 8vo, cloth gilt, 3s. 6d.

East End Idylls

By A. St John Adcock.

"This is a remarkable book   It is a collection of short stories on East End life, but they are told with that real realism of observation of which Mr Morrison has set the fashion.   The setting is real, the slang is real, the manners and customs seem to have been drawn from life."—*The Daily News.*

"It does not need any actual experience of East End life to tell the reader of these 'East End Idylls' that they are the work of a master-hand. . . . The little idylls are all exquisitely done – exquisitely, we say, because there is no other word which will do full justice to the performance."—*The Sun.*

Crown 8vo, cloth gilt, 3s. 6d.

The Dreams of Dania

By Frederick Langbridge,

Author of "Sent back by the Angels," &c.

With Four Full-Page Illustrations by J. B. Yeats.

"Mr Langbridge's novel is one which will be read with unmixed pleasure.   It is sprightly and often amusing, reproducing the talk of Irish peasants and Irish editors.   It is also pathetic, as it gives us with much sympathy and good taste a picture of an Irish rector in sickness and sorrow. . . . Narrated by Mr Langbridge in a manner that holds the interest of the reader from beginning to end.   Bridget is one of the raciest characters in recent fiction, and a novel at once so healthy and so pleasant should be heartily welcomed."—*British Weekly.*

London : 10 *Henrietta Street, Covent Garden, W.C.*

THIRD EDITION.

Fcap. 4to, art canvas, gilt, 3s. 6d.

The House of Dreams

An Allegory

By an Anonymous Author.

"'The House of Dreams' belongs to the same class as Mrs Oliphant's 'A Pilgrim in the Unseen,' and may rival the great popularity of that striking fancy. . . . A book of signal literary beauty, of profound tenderness, and deeply reverent throughout; the work of a man who finds in earth and heaven alike the sign and token of the Cross."—*The British Weekly.*

"A very beautiful allegory. . . . The author's deep reverence and exalted phantasy never ring false, and his work cannot fail to inspire the reader with reverence for ideals undreamed of in worldly philosophy."—*The Pall Mall Gazette.*

Crown 8vo, buckram, 3s. 6d.

The Sorrow of God

And Other Sermons

By Rev. John Oates.

"For the contents of 'The Sorrow of God' we have nothing but praise, and we could wish for nothing more than that the book might be widely circulated. Spiritual insight, large culture, with its consequent breadth of sympathy and eloquent expression, are the distinguishing features of what is, without exaggeration, a collection of notable sermons. . . . Those of our readers who value a fresh utterance on the great problems of religion will lose no time in getting acquainted with a book we have been able to notice all too briefly."—*The Sunday School Chronicle.*

"There are many noble utterances in these sermons. . . . It is because the author helps us to feel purer and better that we so heartily commend his book."—*The New Age.*

London : 10 *Henrietta Street, Covent Garden, W.C.*

THE LAUREL LIBRARY.

VOLUME I.—SECOND EDITION NOW READY.

Crown 8vo, cloth elegant, gilt top, 2s.

Litanies of Life

By Kathleen Watson

Mr T. P. O'CONNOR, M.P., in *The Weekly Sun*

("A Book of the Week.")

" Fancy a woman . . . so gifted, sitting down with the resolve to crush into a few words the infinite tale of all the whole race of her sex can suffer, and you have an idea of what this remarkable book is like. . . . As wonderful an epitome of a world of sorrow as I have ever read."

" So real is this first sketch, so human, so sensitively delicate, so successful in its curious mingling of boldness and tenderness, that the reader necessarily imagines it to be autobiographical, believing that only out of actual sorrow could be distilled so true a record of passion and of regret."—*The Daily Mail.*

VOLUME II.

Crown 8vo, cloth elegant, gilt top, 2s.

The Widow Woman

A CORNISH TALE.

By Charles Lee.

" A delightful little work. . . . Mr Lee knows these fisher folk by heart, and has the ability to draw them to the life in a few bright strokes of drollery. . . . The character sketching is admirable, the scenes and situations are most vividly brought out, and the pervading humour is of a genuine stamp."—*Sheffield Independent.*

" The book is one to read, having the blessed quality of making you chuckle: the best of qualities in literature, one is inclined to say, in these tired days."—*Black and White.*

---

www.ingramcontent.com/pod-product-compliance
Lightning Source LLC
Chambersburg PA
CBHW021214270326
41929CB00010B/1130